Praise for Kay Bratt's Novels

"Kay Bratt beautifully draws the story of a daughter returning to Maui—the enchanted land that she believes holds the key to her past—where she unlocks a promising future she never could have imagined. Full of secrets, love and gorgeous settings, *True to Me* is the ultimate escape." —**Kristy Woodson Harvey, bestselling author of *Slightly South of Simple***

"Heartfelt and brimming with lively characters, *True to Me* is a poignant reminder of the meaning of family, the importance of truth, and the power of forgiveness. Perfect for fans of Christine Nolfi and Cathy Lamb." —**Sonja Yoerg, *Washington Post* bestselling author of *True Places***

"Bratt writes a beautiful tale of family which grabbed me from the very first page. Bratt takes the reader on a heartfelt journey of family and forgiveness while Quinn teaches us about those we should let in and those we should let go. For at the very core of the novel is the rare gift of being true to one's self." —**Rochelle B. Weinstein, *USA Today* bestselling author**

"*Wish Me Home* has all the trademarks of a Kay Bratt novel: a heartwarming story that nourishes the soul, beloved characters, and a plot that kept me turning pages. Without shying away from the harshness of life, Bratt has managed to create a world in which kindness and goodness prevail." —**Karen McQuestion, bestselling author of *Hello Love***

"In this inspiring story of a woman's search for the deepest wish of her heart, Bratt paints a realistic portrait of the dark side of the foster care system, while simultaneously reminding us that there is always hope, and that home and family can be found in unexpected places." —**Kerry Anne King, bestselling author of *Closer Home* and *I Wish You Happy***

"With its resilient protagonist, secret that kept me guessing, dog I wish I could adopt in real life, and story that tugged at my heart, Kay Bratt's *Wish Me Home* grabbed me and held me all the way to its heartfelt resolution. Readers who enjoy novels like Vanessa Diffenbaugh's *The Language of Flowers* will find it a delight!" —**Nancy Star, bestselling author of *Sisters One, Two, Three***

"A baring-of-the-soul emotional story that leaves you with a heart full of love and hope." —**Carolyn Brown**, *New York Times* **bestselling author, for** ***Dancing with the Sun***

"*In Dancing With the Sun*, a mother and daughter are forced to lean on each other for survival in the wilderness while learning to let go of years of grief and guilt. Readers will relate to Kay Bratt's depiction of a mother's love and her courage in protecting her daughter. Ultimately, though, this novel is a page-turner that will pull on your heartstrings and affirm your faith in humanity." —**Karen McQuestion, bestselling author of *Hello Love***

"*Dancing with the Sun* is an evocative story of emotional and physical survival in the harshest of terrains. Mother and wife Sadie Harlan is struggling silently with grief when she and her daughter go missing in Yosemite. Away from the world and focused on keeping her daughter alive, Sadie embarks on an unforgettable journey through loss and guilt to find forgiveness, healing, and strength. Book clubs will love the powerful message of this unique novel." —**Barbara Claypole White, bestselling author of *The Perfect Son* and *The Promise Between Us***

"*Dancing with the Sun* is an endearing, emotional tale filled with the perfect mix of poignant family heartaches, unshakable mother-daughter love, and a dose of adventure in a dramatic, vivid setting that will sweep you away until the very last page. Don't miss it." —**Julianne MacLean, *USA Today* bestselling author**

"Whether facing the natural terrors of Yosemite or the internal pains of an unforgiven past, this mother-daughter story is beautifully written and relatable as one woman faces a mother's greatest fear—losing yet another child. Kay Bratt delivers on all levels in this emotional and tense story of loss and resilience." —**Emily Bleeker, Amazon Charts and *Wall Street Journal* bestselling author**

"Nothing like a harrowing, life-threatening, and completely unplanned hike through Yosemite's backcountry to make you face years of grief and guilt head on. Kay Bratt pulls this off masterfully in *Dancing with the Sun*, an emotional mother-daughter tale of love, forgiveness, and renewal. Book clubs will love Bratt's latest!" —**Kerry Lonsdale, Amazon Charts and *Wall Street Journal* bestselling author**

"In *Dancing With The Sun*, Kay Bratt captures a mother-daughter relationship with an authenticity rarely seen in novels. Highly emotional, heartfelt, and bristling with tension on every page, this is a story not easily forgotten." —**Bette Lee Crosby, *USA Today* bestselling author**

"*No Place Too Far* is Kay Bratt at her best. Free up some time, find somewhere quiet, and dive into this story of Maggie, Quinn, the challenges they face, and the people who love them. Once again, Bratt tackles complex contemporary issues with remarkable agility and compassion, and it's an absolute pleasure to be along for this ride. And because Bratt is a master of location, it's even more of a pleasure when the ride takes place on Maui. For a few brief moments, I forgot all about errands and laundry and the minivan and soaked up Hawaii, in all its glorious heritage and beauty." —**Lea Geller, author of *Trophy Life***

"*No Place Too Far* is the perfect blend of suspense mixed with a magical setting and characters we care deeply about. I loved Maggie and Quinn and rooted for them until the final page. Kay Bratt is a masterful storyteller, and the story's pacing and descriptions of Maui left me always wanting more. Highly recommended for book clubs!" —**Anita Abriel, international bestselling author of *The Light After the War***

"For two women who live in paradise, their lives are anything but idyllic. Best friends Quinn and Maggie have spent the past year trying to outrun dangers from their pasts—one a stalker, the other family secrets. But now both pasts have caught up to them, and the two friends will have to decide if they should keep running or stand up and fight. In this page-turning drama, Bratt has created two strong, dynamic female characters who readers will be sure to root for." —**Amanda Prowse, bestselling author of *The Girl in the Corner***

"In this delicious drama set against the backdrop of

paradise, Kay Bratt weaves a suspenseful story about finding the courage to fight for happiness, forgiveness, and love. I delighted in the enchanting descriptions of Maui, and I rooted for the characters as if they were friends." —**Cynthia Ellingsen, bestselling author of *The Lighthouse Keeper*, for *No Place Too Far***

Caroline, Adrift: Sail Away Series, Book 5

Set sail to new adventures and escapes with eight best-selling authors in the exciting new Sail Away series!

After the death of her beloved James, one woman faces a future of feeling adrift and must find a reason to go on without the love of her life, from the bestselling author of *Wish Me Home*.

When Caroline McClellan's beloved husband passes away, she doesn't know what to do with herself without him as her center and reason for being. Caroline's three adult daughters insist that she accompany them on the cruise that was supposed to mark her fiftieth wedding anniversary. Caroline is a reluctant participant and sure she will not find any joy in a voyage that was supposed to be a celebration but without her husband, feels like a chore.

Betty Martelle is an interesting woman who takes life by the horns and makes it her goal to find purpose in every day that she is still allowed to breathe. Fate will bring a new friend into her life and give her an opportunity to find a way to break through a barrier of grief to share her gift of spontaneity and finding joy in the little things.

Set on a cruise to the lush island of Maui, Caroline, Adrift is an emotional friendship story of two women brought together by fate. One is adrift when it comes to finding meaning in life, and the other is determined to be a beacon of hope and teach her how to do it.

Join Kay Bratt, International Bestselling author, as she brings the latest book in The *Sail Away* series to life, featuring a heartwarming story of love and loss, and the gift of friendship.

Caroline, Adrift

A Standalone Novel

Sail Away Series
Book Five

Kay Bratt

Caroline, Adrift... Copyright © 2022 by Kay Bratt

All rights reserved. No part of this book may be reproduced or transmitted in any form or by any means, electronic or mechanical including photocopying, recording, or by any information storage and retrieval system without the written permission of the author,.except for the use of brief quotations in a book review. For permissions contact the author directly via electronic mail: kay@Kaybratt.com

https://kaybratt.com
Facebook: https://www.facebook.com/KayBratt
Twitter: @Kay_Bratt
Instagram: @Kay_Bratt

Published in the United States by Red Thread Publishing
ISBN 978-1-7363514-7-5
FIRST EDITION
Cover by Elizabeth Mackey Graphic Design

For my wonderful readers in Kay's Kindness Krew

Also By Kay Bratt

Hart's Ridge
Wish Me Home
True To Me
No Place too Far
Into the Blue
All (my) Dogs Go to Heaven
Silent Tears; A Journey of Hope in a Chinese Orphanage
Chasing China; A Daughter's Quest for Truth
Mei Li and the Wise Laoshi
Wish You Were Here
Wishful Thinking
A Thread Unbroken
Train to Nowhere
The Palest Ink
The Scavenger's Daughters
Tangled Vines
Bitter Winds
Red Skies

Caroline, Adrift

By Kay Bratt

Prologue

Mark Twain once said that wrinkles indicate where smiles have been, but Caroline McClellan could only see the harshness of her wrinkles in the reflection of the window and didn't think she'd ever know another smile again. Or at least, not a genuine one. She stood at the kitchen sink, staring out at the yard that was in bad need of some care.

Her eyes were drawn to a sudden flicker of purple, and she saw a hummingbird fluttering around the feeder. It was well after noon, and she was still in her nightgown. She'd just been thinking of something important, but her train of thought suddenly left the station without her.

Oh, the cruise. James' last attempt at humor. Instead of the traditional fancy voyage that most went on for anniversaries, her James had booked them on a cruise for cat lovers and the date was looming. A cruise that was supposed to mark her fiftieth wedding anniversary to her best friend. The man who now lay silent and six feet under the hard earth, four months gone now.

She had a week to go and still had no idea what to pack and no energy to figure it out. Caroline recalled the only other cruise they'd ever taken. It must've been at least thirty years before and the thing that stands out to her now was the way she'd felt like they'd entered a new world when they'd gotten on board. All smiles and handshakes that felt like boarding a place that held an alternate reality. Being the practical person she was, it hadn't set right with her back then and without James to anchor her now, she knew it would feel even more strange the second time around.

The hummingbird dipped in and out, looking for sustenance at the empty container. If James were still alive, it would be clean and full of the perfect formula of sugar and water. He'd always had a way with the hummers. They loved him and every year came in droves. The grandchildren found it magical and thought their Papa was some kind of bird man.

This was the first hummingbird she'd seen in weeks.

She squeezed some dish soap into the sink and turned on the hot water. It felt like a gargantuan task. To her left, the brochure for the cruise glared at her from where James had stuck it to the fridge.

Board A Meow Cruise and Share Your Feline Fervor

Her always comedic husband had thought the idea was hilarious and would be something fun to try. But then, he hadn't known he'd be dead by the time it rolled around, and she'd be left looking like a crazy widowed cat lady.

A cruise to Hawaii—a place that had always been on

his bucket list. And for an additional fee... they would be part of the Meow Mix on board.

She rolled her eyes at the ceiling.

It couldn't be more stupid.

She remembered opening the card and James standing there waiting to see her expression when she saw what he'd written.

We're cruising, babe. This is going to be a life changing trip. Love, James.

She wasn't so sure about life changing. Enjoying anything without him beside her was going to be different, that was for sure, and her life was going downhill fast.

Once the sink was full, she felt another wave of exhaustion and decided the dishes could soak a bit while she flipped the television over to Doctor Oz to see what tips he had to make her feel human again. When she turned to head that way, Felix looked up at her from where he lay curled up on her kitchen table.

"Shoo—get off of there!"

He stared at her, a bored expression across his face.

"Fine. I don't care what you do." Caroline sighed.

The table was off bounds and now that James was gone, their most rebellious cat had taken it over. Next, he'd probably think he had free reign of the counter tops and she'd never be able to have the girls over for dinner again or they'd complain of cat hair in their food—even if they couldn't find one.

His brother, Fauci (named by James during the peak of the pandemic when they thought a new cat would help the boredom of isolation) was the obedient one and was doing his napping elsewhere, curled up like a quiet little fur-angel.

Caroline had always wanted a dog, but the Colorado winters could be harsh, and she didn't want to have to be trekking outside multiple times a day in the cold and snow for potty breaks.

The two felines were enough, and they made quite a pair, one solid black and the other white, bickering with each other often throughout the day and then making up in time for bedtime snuggling. They were opposite in personality. Felix was pure trouble and usually tried to frame Fauci. He stole things from her bedside table or plate, then was famous for taking part of it to his brother and leaving it with him so he'd get the blame when found.

Fauci, on the other hand, had decided since James' death that he was the newly appointed caretaker and had taken over the wake-up-mom-from-nap duty.

Lately Caroline hadn't felt like rising after her usual hour nap, but Fauci somehow sensed when time was up and would come to stand on her chest. There he meowed until she finally relented and climbed out of the bed.

She supposed he was making sure she didn't die, too.

Caroline loved her cats. But she had no plans to compensate for the loss of her husband by adding to the furry entourage. Two was enough, and when they were gone, no more.

And she sure didn't relish the idea of a cat cruise.

She was going to cancel it, but their girls had insisted that she go ahead with the plans. That it would cheer her up and James would've wanted her to go.

"Do it for Dad," they'd begged, then insisted vehemently.

Since Caroline couldn't talk them out of it, she needed to find the energy to look through her closet to see what she could pull together.

She truly did not relish the trip.

At seventy-two years old she had lived long enough to know exactly why her daughters insisted she *do it for Dad*.

Her daughters had more than blue seas and silly themes on their minds.

Most likely, it would be Caroline's farewell tour before they shipped her off somewhere where she wouldn't be their responsibility.

The first alarm bell had gone off when Rachel called to tell her that she and her sisters would be accompanying Caroline and had already booked a room, with plans for one of them to stay in Caroline's cabin with her.

She wondered which daughter had drawn the short straw for that.

That they'd decided to even come was ironic, seeing how for the last ten years her supposedly-mature-adult daughters had refused to be together for anything. Their latest not-on-speaking-terms was over silly stuff, just like always. Something one of them said about the other—or didn't say. Or didn't do. Petty actions that reminded Caroline of when they were children, and one would be upset because the other looked at her for too long.

Caroline remembered one totally inane squabble that Laura and Rachel had over a dish of macaroni and cheese on Thanksgiving at least six or seven years back.

Her oldest, Peggy, always made and brought her famous (to her) crockpot macaroni and cheese, and it was just a given. But when Rachel also arrived with a casserole dish of it that had been baked and tweaked with a different recipe, Peggy claimed it was a passive-aggressive move and had refused to eat a bite of anything on the table. She said her little sister had tried to upstage her. Over macaroni and cheese, for heaven's sake!

Caroline had helped herself to both dishes, scooping out the exact same amount of each and eating every single bite of both, even though she wasn't supposed to have dairy. She'd paid for it that night with intense stomach pains, and her daughters had still refused to speak to each other for months.

It was always something with her girls and over the years, Caroline often wondered what she'd done wrong in raising them. Yes, they did okay for themselves, and some would say quite successfully, but they were so competitive with each other. And one was always mad at the other for something and trying to get the one sister left out of the fuss to choose sides.

There was never a time when all three were getting along at the same time. Caroline couldn't keep up with who was not talking to who.

Yet suddenly here they were, all flowers and rainbows and wanting to vacation together? A burying-the-hatchet reunion could only mean what she already suspected. She wasn't senile. Not yet, anyway, though sometimes she felt they were driving her round the bend at a pace too fast to compute. And she knew her girls better than they knew themselves.

There would be *talks*, there's no doubt about that. Talks about Caroline's future—or lack thereof—now that she was alone and in a big, old house that needed more tender loving care than she was handy enough to give.

Just the week before, her hot water heater had gone on the blink. Caroline tried to take care of it herself and had even set up an appointment with a plumber who was going to install a new one for a fairly good price. Then the girls had gotten wind of it and sent her son-in-law, Scott, who declared it was a simple repair. He'd fixed it, but not without going on and on about saving her several hundred dollars that someone else was sure to have swindled her out of if he hadn't stepped in to *save* her.

She'd never hear the end of it about that blasted water heater. Even James had talked about it needing replaced, so it wasn't like she'd come up with the idea all on her own. So, she could blame it on him.

Not that he'd care, from where he was.

Caroline was quite upset at James, if she was being truthful with herself.

They'd made a pact decades ago that they'd go out of this world together, but he'd broken it when he'd come down with the flu. It wasn't even a week in before a simple bug had turned to double pneumonia that stubbornly set into his lungs.

Before she could even gather her thoughts, he could barely breathe and wasn't even able to tell her what she should do, just in case. Well, in case did happen and she'd had to make all the decisions herself. With help from the girls, of course. Help that came with too much drama.

Even in that they couldn't be united, and Caroline had listened to them bicker over choosing a casket, and what suit he should wear or not wear, and who would do the eulogy.

She had let them fight it out until the funeral director stepped in and guided them toward a resolution and a fitting memorial.

James had always thought funerals were macabre and never fit the person being remembered. He'd told her time and again that he didn't care what she did for him after he died, that he wouldn't be around to critique it.

So, she hadn't cared, either.

Ironically, the number of family and friends who had showed up for him had filled the funeral home and caused a line that wove out the door and around the parking lot. The funeral director said it was unusual to have such a turnout for an older person.

Then again, he hadn't known James, or he wouldn't have been surprised.

The whole depressing event was a blur to her now, other than her insistence that he be buried in his favorite button up shirt and Wrangler jeans, with his lucky fishing pole tucked in beside him. She didn't even remember what was said, or sung, or done.

She could remember, however, just how many grooves were in the first few feet of the coffin that rested in front of her chair, and the nauseating scent of the flowers that smothered and threatened to send her running for the restroom.

It was a miracle, but she'd contained herself and stayed put, though the thought of James right there, within reach, but quietly resting felt surreal to her. The idea that a simple box could contain all that he was—the bawdy jokes, loud laughter, and the sense of security he always gave her—was preposterous.

She'd stared at that casket hard enough that if there was any doubt that the man inside it wasn't dead, he would've popped up and asked everyone what the hell they all were sitting around crying about. Now that would've been a sight to behold and exactly something that her James would do, if he'd had the ability. The next thing out of his mouth would be for someone to hand him a Miller Lite.

Caroline had chuckled to herself at the thought. She'd stifled it under a tissue, because if her girls had heard her, they would've shipped her off to the looney bin for laughing at her own husband's funeral.

She had sobered up quickly when the casket was being lowered into the ground, then flinched as she'd listened to the thuds of shoveled dirt being thrown on top of him. Stifling all chances of it all turning out to be a bad dream. She'd wanted so badly to crawl in there and let them bury her, too.

Being morose wasn't helping anything. She stared out the window. The pile of leaves that he'd left untouched in the yard irritated her and she stared at them. That very day he'd raked them all together she'd told him if he didn't pick them up then, he'd never get to it.

Turns out she was right.

For once, she wished she'd been wrong.

Why hadn't she gone out that day and helped him?

Spent time together when they could get it? Even if she did sneeze like crazy around fallen leaves, they could've made it fun. But she'd watched him from that very window, as though she were a princess in a tower and couldn't deign to come out and do manual labor or at least keep him company while he did it.

Where are you, James? Are you still near? Do you hear me?

The questions were ridiculous, but she couldn't stop asking. She was a logical person (when she wasn't trying to stifle laughter at a funeral), and she knew her husband was gone. He wasn't watching and he sure wouldn't be answering her.

But yes, he would've been the life of the party on the ship.

Without him, Caroline had no idea what to say in a crowd. James was the talker—the social part of their union. She was always just happy to be in his shadow.

She sighed. It wouldn't do any good to keep wishing he was there. That boat had sailed. No pun intended, she told herself. Now she had God only knows how many more years to live on the earth without him.

Felix slipped into a low snore as Caroline left the kitchen to go look through her clothes. But one thing was sure, she wouldn't be packing anything for a formal evening. That's where she'd draw the line with her daughters. They might get her on the ship and make her look like a ridiculous cat-infatuated old lady, but she didn't plan to have one iota of fun and she darn sure wasn't celebrating anything.

Her phone dinged from somewhere in the house and

Caroline turned to go search for it. It took her longer than it should to find it, but the secondary ding helped, and she unearthed it from under the newspaper next to her chair.

It was a text from her youngest daughter, Rachel.

Don't forget to pack good walking shoes in case we do a hike on one of the islands, it read.

Caroline didn't have the energy for a hike around the house to find her phone, much less one on any island. Simply put, she didn't want to do anything, much less take a cruise. She didn't want anything *life changing*, as James had put it. She wanted everything back to the way it was. Either that or she wanted God to go ahead and take her now, so she could be with her husband again.

One

When you get older, your life is supposedly written on your face. If that was the case, Caroline wondered what story hers was telling. Would it be a story of a woman who raised a family and was a devoted wife? Or her trials of teaching hundreds of other people's children, attempting to reach young minds and leave them with lessons to take them through life? Or was it destined to be the tale of a lonely widow who spent her last years with only her cats as company as she pined over the life she'd once had and had left behind?

The day had arrived and now she was on the ship, sitting on a lounge chair, hugging her carry-on bag and pretending not to hear Rachel complain to her sister about the fact that it wasn't fair she was going to have to *sleep with mom*, because their dad had booked a room with a double bed instead of two twins.

"You and Peggy have it made," Rachel whispered loudly. "You each have your own bed and you don't have to make sure Mom takes her medicine or gets up to pee half a dozen times in the night. I'll never get any sleep."

What did they expect? Her daughters thought she and James wanted separate beds on their wedding anniversary? Or ever? She didn't know what gave them the notion that they didn't sleep together anymore but it was ridiculous. And she couldn't wait until their bladders began giving out on them. Then they'd see.

"We should've thought to ask for two beds," Laura said. "There's no way they'll switch you now. The cruise is completely full. You're stuck, but at least you didn't have to pay for your ticket. You can thank Dad for that."

They both glanced at Caroline to see if she was listening, and she looked at the DJ, pretending not to notice. They went back to speaking about her as though she was deaf, too. Ironically, they hadn't even yet seen the cabins and the girls were already complaining. Caroline thought she'd get to go directly there and wasn't pleasantly surprised to find out they may not even be ready before dinner.

"You know she snores at night, don't you?" Laura said.

Caroline resisted the urge to say something, but they weren't talking to her. Only about her. Getting older made you aware of a certain phenomenon that you didn't know about when you were younger. Somehow, being a certain age gave you the superpower of being invisible. Caroline had noticed it probably around her mid-fifties when her looks had suddenly begun to decline at a rapid pace. By sixty, she could walk through stores, into coffee shops, and on any sidewalk in town and feel nearly unseen.

By sixty-five or so, she noticed that at family gatherings, it felt like no one noticed her or cared what she had to say any more. People talked over her if she even tried to contribute to the conversation. They scheduled lake days and other summer outings, rarely asking if she'd like to come, assuming it would be too much for her.

Even if that were true, it would be nice to be asked. She wasn't an invalid.

At first it was disheartening, but she'd always had James to talk to, so it wasn't so bad. They'd joked about it, though, with his boisterous ways and clever conversation, no one ever treated him as though he were invisible. They cared about his stories from his youth with all the escapades he'd gotten himself into because he could tell them so well.

Caroline didn't have that gift, and no one wanted to hear her stories. They probably couldn't imagine that once upon a time, she was young and vivacious, with hopes and dreams just like them. That she had lived through blessings and heartaches, with wisdom that could be shared.

With James gone, she felt like she'd been put on a shelf, set aside to grow old and be lonely. A burden.

"Well, you could trade with me. You're used to not sleeping alone," Rachel said.

Caroline sneaked a peek and nearly laughed at the expression that Laura gave her sister.

"Sleeping with my children is not the same as

sleeping with our elderly mother," she replied, acid dripping from her tongue.

Serves them right. They shouldn't have pushed her to do this cruise thing.

"We should move Peggy in with her," Rachel joked, and they both laughed. "But with her temper, she'd end up throwing Mom over the balcony."

Caroline thought that didn't sound so bad. At least it would all be done with, and she could have some peace.

"Where did Peggy go, anyway?" Laura asked.

"She's probably in the business area, trying to link up to her email because obviously, the world stops turning if she isn't on the internet," Rachel said.

No mother liked to hear their children talk down about each other, and Caroline wished that Rachel and Laura focused on some of their older sister's better qualities. Like how she used to sneak into the kitchen after bedtime when they were kids and returned with enough cookies for all three of them, willing to take the blame all on herself if caught.

Caroline always knew what she was doing but she pretended not to hear because it warmed her heart that her youngest girls had Peggy to look out for them.

Peggy also spent years helping the girls with their homework, teaching them the shortcuts she'd already learned in school, or showing them how to build the best projects and write the most interesting book reports.

Rachel and Laura sometimes banded together in their reluctance to give credit to Peggy for all her big-sister-duties so easily forgotten once they were all out of the house. They didn't understand that Peggy was always simply thinking she needed to look out for everyone. She was born a mother hen and sometimes it just didn't sit well with her independent-minded sisters.

"She may not be able to find us," Laura said. "I didn't expect the decks to be so crowded."

Caroline didn't either. She wasn't used to being around so many people, especially for the last few months after James had left her.

They sat near the pool—one of many and Caroline wasn't even sure what floor they were on. Everything was so confusing, but they'd insisted on coming for the Meow Meet & Greet that the Cat Event Coordinator who had checked them in talked about.

Laura and Rachel had ushered Caroline to the room, then this deck and both now sipped on their free cocktails, a concoction called Meowgaritas and apparently full of tequila.

Caroline had reached for one herself before Rachel had nearly cut her hand off and told the server her mother couldn't have alcohol because of her vertigo. Never mind that Caroline hadn't had vertigo for at least three years and sometimes had a glass of wine at night to help herself get sleepy, but it wasn't worth the argument.

Her free juice was so sweet it was sickening, but she wouldn't say a word. She really just wanted to go to the cabin and unpack, then start counting down days until she could go home.

"Are you in the Meow party?" A young woman approached, carrying a box filled with plastic goody bags. She wore a headband with kitten ears and a t-shirt with a cat on it. A tail swished back and forth from her rear end.

Ironically, the woman's nametag read *Tabby*.

"Yes, she is," Rachel answered before Caroline could speak for herself.

"I don't need the goody bag. Thank you, anyway," Caroline added.

"Mom—yes, you do. We all do. It's already paid for," Laura said, holding her hands out to the woman.

"Names, please?" the woman set the box down and pulled out her cell phone.

Rachel told her their names, and once Tabby verified they were indeed part of the cat crowd, she handed over three small plastic bags.

Caroline set hers on the chair beside her.

"One more for my sister, Peggy," Laura added. "She'll be here shortly."

Tabby gave it to her and smiled widely. "Your bags have your kitten ears and the group shirt to wear during our events, and some nibbles for later. There is also a schedule of events in there with a full list of activities that will be coming up, including our much-anticipated Scaredy-Cat-Scavenger Hunt!"

"Oh, how fun," Caroline said, under her breath, of course.

"Yes, it will be," Tabby said, the sarcasm going over her head. "It's the favorite activity every time. Don't forget to wear your cat shirts."

With that she raised her hand and made like a cat scratching the air, meowed, then moved to the next small group to begin her spiel.

Rachel and Laura returned to talking to each other while they watched the DJ dance like a fool behind his setup, mouthing the words to "Stray Cat Strut," a fresh change from the "What's Up, Pussycat" that had played before it.

It was only the first hour and Caroline was already sick of cat crap—or, um... cat themes. She hoped it would calm down once they got going because after all, were there really people who wanted to take a full cruise only focusing on cats?

Rachel got her phone out and took a selfie with her and Laura, then turned to Caroline.

"Mom, turn your phone on airplane mode," she said. "Or you're going to get hit with roaming fees once we get out to sea."

"I already did that," Caroline said.

"Well, then..." Rachel raised an eyebrow at her. "Aren't you a smartie?"

Laura laughed.

Caroline didn't. She was old, not stupid. And she'd researched online about cruising to get a list of tips, though she wouldn't let the girls know that.

"Did you pack a swimsuit in your carry-on?" Laura asked.

"Nope." She had no plans of swimming and no desire to show anyone her lily-white body. Heck, even she didn't want to see her lily-white body, much less show it to strangers.

"Well, I did, and I'm about to go find a place to change into mine," Rachel said. "Mom, are you going to be okay here if we leave you for a few minutes?"

"I'm sure I'll be perfectly fine," Caroline said. "I'll try not to wander and accidentally fall overboard. And I promise not to accept any marriage proposals from rich Europeans who want to drop a million pounds into my bank account."

"Very funny. Save our chairs, then," Laura said. "We'll be back as soon as we can."

"Take your time," Caroline said, waving them away.

A few rows away from her a woman was already in her pool attire and lying face down on a lounge chair, soaking in the sun. Caroline saw a man approach her, then bend and stick his finger in her ear.

The woman turned over, surprise and then shock turning to anger when the man threw his hands in the air, apologizing and red-faced as he stated he thought she was his wife. He was speaking English, but the woman was yelling back in a foreign language.

Caroline stifled a giggle. It was exactly something that James would've done. More than that, it was something he would've loved witnessing. He was always up for a good laugh.

She pulled her Kindle from her bag and turned it on, going to the book she'd started on the flight to Florida. One paragraph in and she was so startled by the loud ship horn that suddenly blared out, she almost dropped it.

She gathered her things and walked over to the nearest railing and looked out. She realized they were now pulling away from the docks. There was no trembling or real movement. No loud engine noises. Just a slow and surreal slight movement with the land beginning to recede away.

Bon Voyage.

Chapter One

Finally, it was dinner time, and they were sat at a table with two other couples from the Meow roster who immediately showed them photos on their phone of their cats. Caroline had to confess that she didn't have any photos on her own phone, and it made them look at her like she was the Jeffrey Dahmer of cats.

Peggy expertly moved the conversation to something safer and not feline-related.

Damone, their waiter, moved gracefully around the table, filling the water glasses while chatting up the guests. He'd already taken their order for appetizers, and was going to bring wine, too.

Caroline hoped she could get away with a glass or two without the girls lecturing her.

"Would anyone like to order the president's cut of a thirty-six-ounce Tomahawk Bone-In Ribeye from the Indulge menu?" he asked. "It comes with a delicious shallot confit, green peppercorns, baked potato and creamed spinach."

She didn't even make eye contact. She already saw the option on the menu, and it was not included with their meal plan. She wouldn't be splurging, that was for sure.

"I definitely would," one of the guests said.

"It's seventy-five dollars," his wife hissed at him, loud enough for everyone to hear.

He nodded without taking his eyes off the menu. "Yep, I can read. I still want it."

"Great choice," the waiter said. "Anyone else?"

No one spoke up and he moved on to taking orders, one by one.

Caroline chose the grilled salmon and baby potatoes, with summer vegetables. Her mouth watered in anticipation.

Damone finished taking all eight orders and disappeared, leaving behind an awkward silence. The two other couples who made up their table of eight started chatting in a familiar manner, obviously traveling together as friends. They talked about their rooms, marveling over how clean they were, and how easy and uncomplicated the embarkation of the ship was compared to the last trip they'd taken together.

The evening had started out a bit stressful with Peggy upset that she had to wear what she'd traveled in since their luggage hadn't made it to their cabin yet. In solidarity, Caroline and the other girls hadn't changed either, though her own blouse and capris were more suited for a sit-down dinner than Peggy's jeans. Her eldest daughter had finally dropped the subject when Caroline pointed out other guests dressed even more casually than she was and reminded her that it was to be expected on the first night and no one cared.

Peggy wasn't going to relax easily on the trip. Not that it was any surprise.

Rachel and Laura were going with the flow and relieved to just get to dinner at all, considering that there had been a delay and they couldn't be seated until forty-five minutes after their seven o'clock reservation. They'd done a lot of pacing in the outside hallway, after a bit of window shopping in front of the gift shops.

Caroline was happy to finally be off her feet.

Damone returned, balancing a large tray on the edge of the table as he set out the appetizers. Peggy had ordered the Ahi Tuna and Avocado Tower, but Caroline stuck with her two younger girls with a simpler—and safer—tomato mozzarella caprese.

The other four at the table were sharing a variety of things, including a charcuterie board that looked pretty fancy. The description said it was cured pork shoulder, duck rillette, duck pastrami, saucisson, and a hard-boiled Cajun egg with spiced mustard and pickles.

"And I'll be back with more wine in just a minute," Damone said, then backed away.

They all dug in, eager to get something in their stomachs.

"I'm Rosemarie and my husband is Jeff. So where are you all from?" one of the wives asked, turning her attention to Caroline and the girls.

"Colorado Springs," Peggy said, then did the introductions. "And you all?"

"Nevada. We take this cruise once a year."

They moved on, talking about the politics of Nevada and the skiing in Colorado, then the conversation moved back to being on a ship and funny things they'd seen people do.

"Well, this one wasn't funny, but my first husband fell overboard," Rosemarie said, bringing Caroline and the girls to an entranced silence as they waited for the rest of the story.

Her husband nodded emphatically, "She's not kidding, except he didn't fall. He jumped. And I tell her all the time that I'm the better man because I keep sticking it out instead of doing the same thing. She's no picnic to vacation with, let me tell you."

Rosemarie took his comment well, but as she laughed, she jabbed him in the side.

Damone returned with the wine and Caroline pushed her glass toward him. She didn't look at any of her girls, and thankfully, they didn't say anything.

"Was he rescued?" Laura asked, once Damone departed.

Caroline cringed internally, hoping the woman wasn't going to say her ex had drowned.

"Yeah, that's what I want to know," Rachel said. "What's the story?"

"First of all, it was my practice marriage," Rosemarie said, winking at them. "It only lasted a year because we couldn't get along from the get-go. Not sure why I even said yes. We were on a cruise to Cozumel for our honeymoon, and just before we were about to go to bed, we got in an argument while we were on our balcony. He threatened to jump overboard if I said one more word and I told him to go ahead."

"He did it because he couldn't stand to be challenged," her girlfriend said. "Nosedive from the sixth deck."

"He was drunk," Rosemarie said, "and he didn't dive. Just jumped."

"Holy smokes," Peggy said. "Did he get hurt?"

"Unfortunately, no. He was a good swimmer and I tossed him a life preserver, then called emergency. He was picked up ninety minutes later by the crew on a Disney ship that was on the same route. They claim if he hadn't been wearing his white t-shirt under the full moon, they'd have never seen him. Last I heard, he was on his third wife, so that clears me as the aggressor."

Her husband raised his eyebrows, then widened his eyes as though questioning that statement, and Caroline hid the smile that threatened to appear at his very dramatic silent reproach. She was glad Rosemarie didn't see it.

"Is it too nosy to ask what you were arguing about?" Rachel asked. "It must've been really bad for him to get that upset and I'm dying to know what can send a man over a sixth-floor balcony to dark waters below."

The woman smiled. "We were arguing about his choice to wear a white t-shirt to dinner that evening when I'd told him to put on something with a collar!"

They all laughed, and the couples looked so comfortable with each other that Caroline couldn't help but think of how James should be next to her, too. They would've been just one more couple in the dining room, eager to meet new friends and to exchange stories.

Caroline shouldn't keep focusing on what she no longer had. James was gone and she knew it in her heart and soul, and in her head, but she was still getting used to trying to sidestep the pain. To her the deep abyss of grief his name brought on was like a gaping hole in the ground that at first, she kept falling into because she forgot it was there.

"You'd be surprised at how many people fall overboard from cruise ships," Jeff said. "It's somewhat of an interest for me."

"He does research," Rosemarie said, rolling her eyes.

"Since year 2000, more than three hundred," Jeff stated. "But twenty-seven of those were in 2015."

"That's not a huge number considering that more than twenty million people a year go on cruises," Jeff's friend said.

"I guess it's all about perspective," Jeff said. "I think the craziest story I read was about the two twenty-year-olds who were trying to reenact the famous Titanic scene, and both fell off the Princess cruise ship. It took the Coast Guard four hours to find them, and they were lucky to be rescued."

"But they had quite a story for their friends back home," Rosemarie said.

Caroline shook her head. It was unbelievable how careless—and clumsy—people could be. She was suddenly glad they'd never cruised as a family with three daughters. It was hard enough keeping up with her girls when they'd stayed on solid ground during holidays.

The conversation continued easily, now that the ice was broken with such a fantastical story, and Caroline was enjoying herself, even if the marital banter sometimes hit a tender spot for her. There was so much going on in the dining room all around them that it was easier to let the activity occupy her thoughts, so they didn't wander too far into lonely territory.

It made her feel proud to see her daughters being such good dinner partners, their charm and manners on display as they chatted, and maybe even boasted a bit about their lives, but in totally appropriate proportions. Caroline got to hear updates about all her grandkids, the girls telling strangers more of a rundown than they ever did her, their own grandmother. However, they were being respectful of her in front of the others, and that meant a lot. Nothing was more embarrassing than to have your adult children try to mother you or treat you like a child in front of strangers.

Damone and another waiter returned with their dinner plates and set them out. Her salmon looked utterly perfect, and one bite in told her the taste matched. The baby potatoes just about melted in her mouth, and she realized that she hadn't had a nice meal in quite a while. It was just easier to eat small, simple things and not put any effort into cooking for one. The delicious assortment of flavors dancing across her taste buds made her realize how much she missed good food.

"Okay, I've got another good story to share," Rosemarie's husband said, putting down his fork. "This one is about an old man who lives in Idaho. He wrote a letter to his son in prison, lamenting his absence because without him, he was going to have a really hard time planting his potatoes this year, and asked if there was any chance of early release."

They all waited.

"Well, the old man got a letter back from his son telling him not to dig up the garden—because that's where he'd buried all the guns! Then after the letter came, a full police force showed up and dug up the garden and found nothing. A week later, the man got another letter from his son that apologized for not being there to help, but that was the best he could do."

They all laughed.

The two couples were going to be fun dinner companions and Caroline was glad they'd be placed with them throughout the cruise. She listened at yet another story opening, then focused on her food, her daughters, and to enjoying the rest of the evening.

Two

Caroline sipped her coffee and looked out over the ocean, watching the morning sunlight skip across the water in a twinkling and hypnotic dance. In every direction all she could see was sky and water. So very much water. It made her feel small and insignificant, giving her an epiphany that the world and the universe was bigger than she'd ever imagined.

Truly unmeasurable.

Of course, she was also thinking of James, and how much he would've loved to be there and how wonderful it would be to have her best friend there with her. She felt a wave of longing, then irritation at herself. Nothing would bring him back, so she needed to stop wishing.

Laughter floated over her, and she looked to see where it came from. She saw a family seated together, parents and three children. The kids looked sunburned but happy, and Caroline was reminded of the first time they had taken a family vacation to Myrtle Beach. They'd stayed at a gated community—called a campground but had tons of beach houses, too— and for the whole week they used a golf cart to get around. Mornings were slow and easy, afternoons spent at the beach playing and swimming, and evening cooking their meals on the porch grill.

James thought he was the barbeque king and took care of the main dish each night. Caroline and the girls worked together in the kitchen for side dishes, and they laughed and got along so well that week. The place had a small water park and James wore his legs out escorting Rachel up the long flight of stairs to the main waterslide a gazillion times a day so that she could do what her big sisters were doing. She was too afraid to do it alone, and Laura and Peggy thought she was too slow, so James was her water pal.

He'd never complained. He always took his Daddy Duty very seriously.

Caroline was always at the bottom of the slide, ready with the camera to get good shots of the girls when they splashed through to the bottom. Somewhere were a ton of photos, but she wasn't in a lot of them because she was the one who took them.

Now all photos were digital, it seemed. Never printed out to hold in your hand or to stick to the refrigerator. If she wanted to see a current picture of her grandchildren, she had to use a device or go look at the framed school shots that were at least a few years old.

A glint of light on a board a few feet across the deck caught her attention and she squinted to see what it was.

When she still couldn't tell, she rose and walked over to it, thinking it might be a lost ring, or pendant.

It was a dime.

She picked it up and held it in her hand. Without her glasses, she couldn't tell the date on it, but the fact that she was just thinking of James and then saw a random dime on the floor didn't go over her head.

James was an avid coin collector, and his favorite collections involved his dimes.

A huge coincidence, to be sure, but that was all. Caroline didn't believe in any sort of woo-woo spirits-are-watching nonsense.

She slipped the coin into her pocket and rejoined the girls at the table.

They hadn't even noticed she'd walked away and returned.

It was going to be a sea day, meaning they wouldn't be pulling into any ports. It was just as well, as she hoped to be able to squeeze a long nap in before dinner. She poked at her fruit. She'd decided to keep it safe to avoid stomach issues, but the pineapple slices were delicious.

"Those look delicious," she said, pointing to salted caramel pancakes on Laura's plate.

"That's a lot of gluten and sugar," Peggy remarked. "We've gone to totally clean eating in my house. Those pancakes wouldn't fly."

Laura took a huge bite and waved her fork at her sister, scowling. "Too bad my household is *dirty*-eating. But then, some of us can't afford a housekeeper who doubles as a cook and can take the time to create such healthy meals. Oh wait—some of us can't even afford the cost of eating clean."

Caroline cringed. This was always a sore subject. Laura had three young children and barely hung on most weeks with juggling them back and forth to school and events while working a full-time job as a branch manager at the bank. Her husband, Grant, worked as a lineman with the power company and was sent out of town a lot, leaving Laura to act as a single parent more times than not. Caroline had stepped in to help them by being their childcare many times over the years, though now all the kids were in school and after-school activities, so they didn't need her.

Peggy, on the other hand, had already gone through everything Laura was going through now. She was further into her career as a realtor, her kids were teenagers with jobs, and her husband, Scott, was a general manager of a telephone company. As an executive, he could make his own hours and had a ton of flexibility. They were overall more financially secure and settled than Rachel's family.

Caroline had a feeling that Peggy conveniently forgot all the scraping it took to get where she is now, and she had a bad habit of passing along unsolicited life-coaching advice, a gesture that irritated both her sisters. Even Rachel, who was willingly single and even more willingly, without children. She was a free spirit, happy to be exploring the world unencumbered and uncounseled. She didn't want anyone telling her what to do or how to do it.

Peggy gave Laura a disgusted look. "Well, it costs nothing to use your manners, but you choose not to. Why don't you close your mouth while you're eating?"

The other two also thought Peggy had a touch of superiority, though Caroline knew her eldest daughter didn't have an elite bone in her body. She did the things she did and said the things she said to camouflage her lifelong self-consciousness and need to please. Peggy came off as confident to most people, but she couldn't fool her own mom. It was a façade.

"Please, girls. It's a bit too early for squabbling, don't you think? At what age are you going to act like adults?"

Laura glared at Peggy one more time, then concentrated on her pancakes.

"Mom, that fruit is a good choice, but the benefits will be gone in an hour or two. You need to at least have some oatmeal and granola," Peggy said, her voice suddenly syrupy sweet. "I'll go get you some."

She didn't wait for an answer as she rose from the table and briskly walked to the buffet line, probably to give her a chance to step away from Laura.

"Gawd...she is *so* bossy," Laura said. "She thinks because she's the oldest that she should be in charge, and she thinks everything she does is perfect. If you wanted oatmeal, you would've gotten it. Your legs work."

She was right. Caroline didn't want oatmeal. Or granola. But she'd eat it. Peggy meant well.

"Just try to get along, please. For me," Caroline said.

"Do you think Rachel will be coming to eat? Should I go check?" Peggy looked concerned.

She was obviously going to ignore the plea about her sister.

"No. She said don't wake her," Caroline replied.

The night before was restless, to say the least. She had to give it to Rachel, her youngest daughter, who had tried to stay in a good mood as they'd retired for the evening. She'd even decided to skip any entertainment on their first night so that they could rest up.

After they'd finally unpacked and tried to find places for all their things, with Rachel taking over the limited space on the tiny bathroom counter, leaving Caroline to use the desktop area for her own makeup and creams, they'd crawled into bed.

Caroline hadn't slept with one of her children for decades and the supposedly queen-size bed sure didn't give them much room for personal space. It occurred to her as they each tried to move the farthest they could get to their sides of the bed, that it shouldn't feel so awkward. For goodness' sake, they were family.

Rachel was her youngest and had grown up more attached to Caroline than the other two girls. Or perhaps it was the other way around and Caroline knew she was the last, so had held on to her a little tighter. She loved them all the same amount, of course, but they each needed a different kind of mothering. Rachel was a dreamer, always flitting from one career to another, and currently trying to make it as a professional photographer. Caroline and James had helped her financially more than the others. It seemed their youngest was always getting into a money pinch.

Caroline's tight bond with Rachel had lasted

through elementary school and then on through high school, when one particularly hard breakup with a boy had landed Rachel in her bed for weeks. Together they'd consumed embarrassingly heavy amounts of ice cream and binge-watched the shows that Caroline didn't really care for but gave her daughter some comfort as she coached her through the tears and regrets that first breakups always caused.

James had spent those weeks on the couch and hadn't minded a bit. He'd never known how to handle 'girl stuff' as he'd called it and was thankful that Caroline always found a way to get their daughters through the many emotional crises that girls tended to have.

Now he was gone, and Caroline was wondering where the closeness with Rachel had gone that made it feel like she was sharing a bed with a stranger.

Rachel must've felt the same because she'd been unusually quiet. Their first hour in was fine. Then her daughter had woken her a few times to tell her to turn over, that she was snoring. Caroline never could sleep well on her side, and she'd lain awake for hours trying to be quiet but feeling like a prisoner in the tight little cabin with the small, confining bed.

"Dad would really be enjoying breakfast if he were here," Laura said, breaking the awkward silence.

"He sure would've. His plate would be heaping full of all the things that irritate Peggy, and he'd probably have an extra tower of bacon," Caroline said, smiling over her mug. "Breakfast was his favorite meal of the day."

Laura groaned. "I hope she isn't going to keep judging me the whole trip."

Peggy returned with a bowl of oatmeal topped with granola and a spoon.

"This will hold you over until lunch," she said as she placed it in front of Caroline.

"Thank you." She rarely ever ate in the mornings, and her daughters would know that if they ever came over for anything other than holidays.

"What are we going to do today?" Laura said, looking from Caroline to Peggy.

"I've got to attend to some emails, but I should be done by noon," Peggy said stiffly. "Then I'd like to work on my tan."

"Mom?" Laura raised her eyebrows. "They've got Bingo on board. Also, Trivia."

"Hmm... I don't know. Let's see what Rachel wants to do," Caroline said. She was relieved that they didn't mention the Meow group. Their activity sheet said today was a Meow Meet & Greet Luncheon after the Cats & Coffee Breakfast for early risers. She'd seen a few ladies wearing the cat ears and had pretended not to notice them all gravitate to a few tables to the side.

"Oh," said Peggy. "I didn't know we were all going to hang together. And I think Rachel said something about taking a fitness class. Or maybe it was dance. I don't know. I just thought we were all going to kind of do our own thing until tonight. I planned on trying the surfing simulator machine but Mom, you can't do that."

"Right. But what's tonight?" Caroline asked.

"Theatre. They're doing *Grease* and we can all enjoy that."

"I hope they have great singers," Laura said. "I know every word to every song."

"Don't we all?" Peggy said, then they both laughed.

Caroline smiled. "You sure do. This will be great for all of us. Remember all the *Grease* parties that you girls had? You'd watch the movie over and over, singing and dancing, and fighting over who would be Sandy."

"Usually Peggy," Laura groaned. "Because she had the blonde hair and she thought she did the accent better than us."

"Not just because of that," Peggy argued. "Rachel wanted to be Rizzo because she liked her attitude. And you were Frenchie, right? You loved doing hair."

"I didn't love doing hair. I was always Frenchie because you always insisted on being Sandy," Laura said. "And you're still bossy."

They glared at each other across the table.

Caroline stood, placed her spoon next to her bowl of half-eaten oatmeal, and gathered her bag. She looked down at her grown-but-acting-like-children daughters.

"I'm going for a walk."

Laura started to stand, and Caroline held her hand up to stop her.

"Alone. I'll catch up later." With that, she turned her back and left them at the table while she contemplated which banister to throw herself over.

Caroline knew from experience—hers and the witnessing of others through the years—that families were just messy and sometimes the best you could do is to remind each other that blood is forever, and it was best to try to keep it from spilling. But she had to give the girls credit, they'd come together for the evening showing of *Grease* and had even seemed to enjoy each other's company. It made her happy and gave her hope that maybe the cruise was a good idea, after all.

They stood for the well-deserved standing ovation.

"That was fantastic," Caroline said. "It really took me back. And wow—the cast was superb, weren't they?"

"They sure were," Rachel agreed. "I thought the show would be lame but now I wish it had lasted even longer. I'd love to see the final scene again."

"Well, me too, except I don't think I can wait much longer for the lady's room," Caroline said, laughing quietly. "I shouldn't have had that Maui Sunrise cocktail."

"Mocktail, you mean," Rachel said. "You might have to pee, but I guarantee you don't have the buzz that mine gave me."

"Now what?" Peggy said as they settled back into their seats to wait for the crowd to thin out a bit before leaving. She talked as she peeked at her phone. "Anyone up for a drink in the piano bar?"

"I can't. I'm going to try to call the kids," Laura said. "Grant sent me an email that Emily won't speak to him because he forgot to bring her soccer cleats to practice, and she had to sit out. He claims it was my fault because I didn't put it on his task list."

"Can't Emily remember her own cleats?" Peggy asked. "I mean, she's plenty old enough to have some responsibility and it's a good time to practice now before she goes to high school and things like that really affect her school performance and thereby, her future transcripts. It'll be good for her if she has to sit out because of it."

Laura ignored Peggy's comment and looked at Caroline. "Now I'm worried he won't remember to take snacks to Olivia's class on Wednesday like I promised. I don't even know if I wrote that one down, either. If he does remember, he'll probably take something silly like fruit snacks or cupcakes and embarrass Olivia. Oh man... I should've never attempted to take a vacation without them. The girls are going to have me tarred and feathered when I get home."

"Oh, they'll be so glad to have their mom home that they'll forget all about it," Caroline said.

"I seriously doubt that," Laura said. "I'll be making it up to them for the next year."

"I'll go for a nightcap, Peggy," Rachel said. "Maybe they'll actually have some men in there who still have all their teeth and aren't wearing white socks with their loafers."

Caroline laughed. James used to do that, too. It seemed the older a man got, the less he cared about fashion choices. And the older their wives got, the less they wanted to point it out.

"I really doubt there are any worthy candidates for you on this boat, dear girl," she said. "You'd need a singles cruise to find that."

Rachel and Laura laughed.

"Mom, no one goes on cruises to look for dates. We

have apps for that," Rachel said. Laura was nodding dramatically beside her. Peggy had her nose in her phone.

Caroline shrugged. "I'm just saying."

"If I'm lucky, maybe our roughed-up Danny Zuko wanna-be will decide to have a drink, too," Rachel said. "It wouldn't hurt to run into him and see if those muscles he displayed on stage are real. I mean, if he's not gay."

"That's rude and you're stereotyping," Peggy said. "Not every stage actor is gay, you know."

Laura rolled her eyes to the ceiling. "Get off your soapbox, big sister. It was a joke. I'll walk Mom to her room. You two go on ahead."

Caroline was just about to say that she'd go for a nightcap, too, after stopping by to use the bathroom, but Rachel cut in.

"Don't worry, Mom, I'll be quiet when I come in but try to stay on your side of the bed," Rachel said.

They probably didn't want their elderly mother tagging along anyway. She'd already spent most of the day wondering where they were and what they were doing. She'd read for a few hours up on the Lido deck, then got lost trying to find her room and reluctantly had to go to guest relations to ask, and then be led there as though she were a wandering Alzheimer's patient from a nursing home. The ship was just so big and the little fish on the carpet didn't help her one bit in finding which hallway was theirs.

The girls had insisted the trip was going to be good for them to all be together, but obviously they only meant in spurts.

Caroline swallowed her disappointment and stood, ready to go. She doubted she'd be asleep when Rachel came in, no matter how late it was, as insomnia now seemed to want to be her best friend. That's why a real nightcap would've been great to settle her down and maybe even tire her brain out a bit more. She was having the same problem at home, always feeling sleepy but not tired because she didn't have enough to monopolize the long hours of the day.

She remembered reading in the cabin brochure something like, *"on this adventure you will get to do something you haven't done in a very long time, which is 'Absolutely Nothing.'* The problem was, Caroline had absolutely nothing to do every day, especially now that James was gone, and she no longer filled the hours with taking care of him.

The rest of her life seemed impossibly empty and much too full of doing nothing. She truly didn't know what the point was any more.

"Yes, Rachel," she murmured. "I'll stay on my side and try not to snore."

"You need to get rested up for tomorrow when we dock at Honolulu," she replied. "You and the cat cruisers have a big day planned at the Aloha Tower."

Caroline sighed. She'd tried not to think about that. She wasn't feeling social enough to interact with strangers and would've rather just stayed with her daughters on the outing. They'd informed her they had planned some hikes and didn't think she could physically handle them, so had signed her up to go with the group, without even asking her.

"Don't forget to wear your cat ears headband," Peggy said. "It's required."

She followed them down the aisle toward the exit, now eager to get one more night over with so she'd be that much closer to getting home to her nothing-filled future.

Three

It was ironic to Caroline that she'd always heard that everyone wants to live a long life, but once they were almost there, the idea of getting old was no longer appealing. The human spirit wanted it both ways, yet they had no idea what they were asking for and from her current view, it was never a more fitting conundrum to think about.

Her life had played out stuck in fast forward, right before her eyes, in a speed that felt like something out of a movie. It seemed like just yesterday she and James were married, then had the girls, and were busy with juggling everything that families did. The seasons and years flew by and now here she was a widowed grandmother, looking at living the rest of her life alone.

How could that even be?

She followed behind the group, trying to not look as though she were a part of the assembly of bodies that like her, were all in some stage of disintegration, but who had plastered their best *we can do this* expressions across their faces. They all wore the mandatory cat shirts, and most of them wore their cat ear headbands.

"Oh, you forgot your cat ears," the director of the group said at the head count before they'd disembarked. "I can get you a new pair."

"No, that will be fine. Putting things on my head makes it hurt," Caroline said. It wasn't true but she was not going to stoop to putting silly ears on and make an even bigger fool of herself.

Once off the bus they were greeted by two beautiful Hawaiian girls who put colorful leis around their necks and told them aloha. A few of the men in the group chuckled and made jokes about getting laid, and their wives shushed them.

Men were just teenagers in old bodies, it seemed.

"Thank you," Caroline said when she got hers, then moved along to where Tabby, their director, was waving to them.

She was in full action mode and Caroline didn't know what kind of medication she was on, but she was entirely too happy to be leading such a group of misfits. Even so, Caroline had to give her respect, as she never showed a bit of disappointment in her job.

Tabby led them into the marketplace courtyard and stopped at a statue of a hula girl.

"The Aloha Tower is one of Hawaii's most iconic symbols," she said. "Built in 1926, it's more than eighteen stories tall and once upon a time its lighthouse served as a navigation landmark from sea and during the World War II it was painted camouflage. The tower has welcomed visitors for nearly a hundred years, since way back when visiting Hawaii was only possible if traveling by steamer ship."

That was interesting. Caroline imagined how excited people back then must've been to see the tower and be able to get off the ship to explore the island. Most likely they would've had to travel the sea much longer on the slower ships and were ready to be on solid ground.

"There used to be more than thirty stores and lots of restaurants and street side cafes here," Tabby said. "It started to flounder, and the university saved it, so you'll see many of the old shops and restaurants have been converted to conference or classrooms. But there's still a few places open to pick up an iconic Hawaiian shirt, a ukulele, or any number of souvenirs. And if you don't see what you like here, you'll get another chance to shop for trinkets tomorrow when we are in Maui. We'll be on the famed Front Street, and it's got plenty to choose from."

Caroline wasn't really into shopping, but she wouldn't mind something cold to drink so she separated from the group to go find a shop.

"Once we get inside, you can all split up or stay together, whatever you prefer, but meet me back here at this statue at one o'clock to catch the trolley for our city tour. And don't forget to take the vintage elevator to the observation deck in the tower," Tabby called out. "You can catch a wonderful view from there."

That sounded like a better plan and Caroline switched directions to head there first and beat the rest of the group who were on a mission to snatch up their souvenirs first.

Just before she was out of earshot, she heard a woman in the group exclaim over a poster in one of the shop windows advertising flowered rain jackets for only fifty dollars.

"I can get those cheaper in the US," she remarked loudly.

"You *are* in the US," the woman next to her said. They both burst out laughing.

Between that comment and the one a few minutes earlier when she'd overheard another guest ask Tabby if she knew what time they served midnight buffet on the ship, Caroline couldn't get away fast enough. She approached the elevator area and saw it was indeed very vintage with a very narrow set of doors and an antique indicator over the top that had a bronze arrow to point to what floor the elevator was currently on.

I hope it's not so old it falls.

She pressed the button and waited, then stepped on when the doors opened.

"Lord don't leave me now," she muttered as it rode slowly to the top against a background chorus of levers and pullies creaking and whining.

It made it and she stepped out. She saw four balconies with *Aloha* etched into them looking out in each direction. She chose the one pointed over the harbor. It was indeed a brilliant view, and she could see their ship and crew who were taking advantage of the decks being nearly empty as they scurried around to clean.

She went to a different balcony that faced downtown and it was interesting, at least what wasn't blocked by the skyscrapers and hotels. It would've been amazing to see it back when no other buildings were allowed to be built taller than the tower.

The elevator dinged behind her, but Caroline didn't turn.

She walked to another balcony and saw a runway. She watched a commercial airplane take off and then immediately veer to the right to avoid flying over the city. Then suddenly she saw not one, or two, but five military planes take off in quick succession! They didn't have to make the quick turn one way; they flew straight up.

That right there would've made James' whole trip. He loved to see and talk about military aircraft.

She looked out and wondered where the girls were. When they'd left her to her own devices on the ship the day before, Caroline had felt like she was in a fog, but she'd put on a brave face and played a few rounds of Cat-Trivia Bingo. Didn't win anything.

Then she'd walked around a few of the shops on the ship but didn't see anything she needed or could afford.

Finally, she'd gone back to the cabin to rest alone, but their housekeeper was there.

She'd apologized and tried to leave but Caroline talked her into staying and cleaning around her. Not that she wanted fresh sheets or towels folded into cute little animals, but it was nice having someone to talk to. A regular person and not someone forcing a paid-for-smile.

Inger, the housekeeper, told her she was from Norway and was working on cruise ships in order to save enough money to send her only son to university, as she called it. He was only seven but as she was a single parent

—he was being watched by his grandparents—she needed to start early to put that money aside.

Caroline watched her face light up when she talked about her son, and her dimples shined. She was a very beautiful young woman, and such a hard worker. It was heartbreaking that she had to be away from him and her homeland for so many months at a time.

When she'd finished cleaning the bathroom, she'd ducked out the door and left a shadow of loneliness in her wake, until Rachel had finally returned, busting in like a cyclone to get ready for dinner.

None of the three girls had asked her how she'd spent her day.

A gust of wind picked up and Caroline turned into it just in time to get slapped in the face with a piece of paper that blew up from the concrete floor.

She pushed it off, then grabbed it before it fell again.

Across the top it read, **March For Babies: A Mother of a Movement**

The next line stated it was an upcoming March of Dimes walkathon at the Kapi`olani Park to raise funds for babies in NICU and other child-related causes.

Feeling irritated that she could've lost an eye from the sharp corner of the paper, she took it to the trash bin and put it in. Nothing irritated her more than littering. Well —actually there were a lot of things that irritated her more, but still, it wasn't nice to get slapped in the face unexpectedly. Quite embarrassing, actually.

She could see a woman in her peripheral view, assumingly the one who had stepped off the elevator after she did, and she hoped her wrestling match with the flying paper wasn't seen. She headed for the elevator, hoping to just slip away.

"Hello," the woman called out.

Caroline sighed, then turned to her.

"Hello."

"How did you like the view?" the woman asked.

She was a good bit older than Caroline.

Caroline couldn't see her eyes behind the big sunglasses and under the hot pink visor she wore. She was Asian, her perfectly coiffed hair a lovely gray with a few dark streaks remaining, and she wore a colorful flowered top over soft-pink pants. It was quite a fashion statement, but in a very well put together way. It was obvious that she had the natural ability to style herself that Caroline had always wished she had.

And here she was, wearing a ridiculous Cat Cruiser t-shirt.

"It's nice," Caroline said. "I saw some military planes take off a few minutes ago."

The woman nodded. "And wait just five more minutes and we'll see them again. They've increased training and operations here since the heightened tensions with China. They're bringing in more planes and drones to get ready for longer missions around the Pacific."

"Oh." Caroline didn't stay abreast of politics, so she had nothing to contribute to the subject.

"I'm Betty Martelle."

"Caroline."

"I see you're with the cat group," Betty said, looking at her shirt. "I think I just saw most of them headed down the street. You can probably still catch them."

Caroline shrugged. "I'm not really a group kind of person. It wasn't my idea to sign up to the Meow part of the cruise."

Betty smiled. "Being with a group has its advantages, especially if you don't like to be alone. I'm on the same ship as you are, but without a group."

"Oh, you're cruising alone?"

"I am, but I'm used to it. I do this cruise three times a year. Sometimes I bring a friend, but this one didn't fit into anyone's schedule back home."

"Where is back home?"

"San Francisco. It's a gorgeous place to live, but you sure don't see views like these from there. Where are you from?"

"Colorado. No ocean views there at all. But did you say you take this exact cruise three times a year?"

Betty nodded. "Sometimes on a different cruise line or ship, but always this path. I have family on Maui and it's a much more fun way to drop in for a few days. I get to immerse myself in the fantasy ship life, visit my Ohana for a few days on Maui, then return to San Francisco feeling refreshed and caught up on family business."

Caroline tried not to show her surprise. Betty must be filthy rich because cruising wasn't cheap. She and James had cut corners for nearly a year and then it still had taken a big chunk of their savings to pay for theirs. She wished now she had stood her ground and canceled the trip and gotten at least a partial refund. The mother-daughter time the girls had insisted they needed wasn't really panning out that way so far.

"Well, it was nice meeting you," Caroline said. "But I suppose I'd better be going."

She checked her phone to see if any of the girls had texted or tried to call to check on her.

Nothing. But then, they thought she was with the group.

"Oh, are you going back to the ship?" Betty asked.

Caroline paused. She really wasn't sure what to do. Going back to the ship alone didn't sound too appealing. Following the Cat Cruisers around didn't either.

"I know a lot about the islands," Betty said. "If you'd like, we could do our own little walking tour. Nothing major—or we could even just go somewhere for a glass of wine. Wait out the next few hours until it's time for you to meet your group."

She looked so hopeful that Caroline couldn't really come up with a good reason to turn her down. It also felt nice to be wanted.

"Sure, that sounds like fun."

Betty clapped her hands together and smiled brightly. "Oh, this is just wonderful. I do so like to make new friends and I love to share about the Hawaiian history. I know just the place to start."

Caroline followed her into the elevator and Betty chattered all the way down and out of the complex and kept on as she guided them to the sidewalk. She told Caroline of her history and how her Chinese great-grandfather had landed on Maui and made his fortune there with the sugar plantations before marrying a Hawaiian young woman.

They walked for about ten minutes before Betty stopped at the gates of a majestic building. It boasted towering columns that flanked a wide veranda across the front.

"This is the Iolani Palace," she said. "It was the seat of royal power after King Kamehameha III moved the capital here from Maui in 1845. The royal family lived here for eight generations."

"It's huge," Caroline said. "Can we go inside?"

"Sure can. They give guided tours and audio tours, or we can just walk around, and I'll give you the highlights."

"The highlights sound good to me."

"Perfect," Betty said. "That way we can talk about other things, too."

They went to the ticket booth and paid, then began their long walk up to the entrance.

"This is the only royal palace on US soil that has been a territorial capitol, a military headquarters, and a prison for a queen," Betty said. "And it had electricity even before the White House. The King wanted everyone around the world to know he and his people were forward-thinking and progressive."

Caroline raised her eyebrows. "Sounds like a captivating story. Are you sure you aren't a tour guide in disguise?"

Betty laughed. "I probably could be! Feel free to tip. Seriously, though, I'd get bored, I'm sure. Visiting a few times a year is enough for me."

They entered the building and Caroline was struck

silent at the opulence. The floors were covered with a carpet of delicate blue with periwinkle and white flowers and led the way to a monstrous stairway that was the focal point of the room.

"The staircase is made of Hawaiian koa wood and leads to the family suites on the second floor," Betty said. "It's quite something, isn't it?"

Caroline could only nod.

"Come, I'll show you some of the more interesting rooms."

Caroline followed and Betty talked as she led her first to a large room decorated in crimson and gold, called the Throne Room, where the king held court in front of audiences and diplomats, and held lavish balls. Then they went through the Blue Room, the Music Room, and the State Dining Room with windows from floor to ceiling and a table set with crystal and porcelain dishes and glasses.

Betty rattled off tons of interesting tidbits as they wandered through King Kalakaua's private suite, then stopped at a room called the Imprisonment Room.

"After the King died, he was succeeded by his sister Queen Liliuokalani who was fifty-three years old when she was crowned. After there was an insurrection to attempt to restore the monarchy, she was arrested for treason and went through a humiliating public trial, then was made to yield to authority to avoid great loss of life of her people. They kept her under house arrest in this room for nine months. She was allowed to see no one, other than one lady-in-waiting."

Caroline walked over to the focal point of the room,

a large case-like table that held a colorful quilt under glass.

"She did this?" she asked.

Betty nodded. "She kept herself busy with quilting and crocheting. She also composed music and was a gifted songwriter, penning over one hundred sixty songs over her lifetime, most of them sad. One of her songs is famous throughout the world and has been sung by many famous people over the decades."

"What was is it called?"

"Farewell to Thee," Betty said. "Even Johnny Cash covered it in his own version."

Caroline was in awe as she looked around the room and imagined day after day, wondering what your fate would be and marveling how the Queen had been able to accomplish anything as she waited—much less make beautiful art and compose songs. It was mind-boggling.

"Another surprising fact about the queen was that she married an American. He was the son of a Boston sea captain and had met her at school when he knew her simply by her given name, Lydia. It sounds like a fairytale story, but their marriage wasn't happy. She couldn't give him children and he eventually fathered a child with one of her servants. The queen adopted the child and later, three more. But her husband died only a few months into her very short reign."

"Sounds like she led a tragic life," Caroline said.

"She did, but even after being overthrown she continued to do mighty things for her people. She never let age define her and kept up a busy life long into her late years. She would be pleased to know that even though her kingdom was annexed and swallowed up by the United States, a hundred years after the overthrow, President Clinton signed a Congressional resolution in which the US government formally apologized to the Hawaiian people."

Caroline felt a flicker of guilt. She didn't even know or understand what all had been done to the Hawaiian people, but obviously it was enough that it warranted an apology.

"I'm so sorry," she offered.

Betty smiled softly. "Apology accepted. Now let's go look at the amazing dresses on display. Just wait until you see her coronation gown. It's phenomenal. Queen Liliuokalani was a force to be reckoned with, but just like any girl, she did love her fashion."

Caroline laughed and followed Betty out of the Imprisonment Room, leaving the air of tragedy behind them.

Four

Betty insisted on treating Caroline to an early dinner to thank her for being her friend for the day, and by the time they arrived at Azure, Caroline was exhausted from walking and couldn't be seated fast enough. She felt discouraged at herself because she was loving the afternoon and wished her body could keep up with her brain.

"My feet are killing me, but my hips are competing for the honor," Caroline said, slowly easing herself into the chair. It was instant relief to her feet. "This getting old stuff is for the birds."

"Now, now. You can't let aging get you down," Betty said. "It's too darn hard to get back up!"

They both laughed at that, and the serious moment was broken. Betty was like a fresh breath of air to be around.

The hostess sent them along with a young waitress and told her to seat them at table ten, which ended up being outdoors, overlooking a gorgeous view.

Betty was also a wonderful tour guide, and Caroline felt so much more knowledgeable about Hawaiian history. She also felt lucky to have run into Betty at the top of the tower because she'd barely thought about the girls in several hours.

"If you'll allow and don't have any dietary restrictions that I need to know about, I'd like to order for us both. I don't want you to miss the Wagyu steak or the truffled creamed corn. Though you may not like the beef lotus dish, as it's more of an acquired taste," Betty said.

"I can eat anything, and I'll go with whatever you choose. I'm just thankful to be here. But if we're having steak, you have to let me pay for my own."

"Not a chance. Today you are my guest."

Caroline wasn't comfortable with someone else paying her way, but she couldn't think of how to get out of it without being rude. When their waiter, Tom, came to the table, Betty ordered.

"So, tell me," Betty said after the waiter left. "What brought you on the cruise?"

"It's for my fiftieth wedding anniversary."

"Oh." Betty looked confused.

"My husband James died a few months ago and I wanted to cancel the cruise, but my three daughters made me come anyway," Caroline said. She hesitated, told Betty the rest of the story, then buttoned it up with why she was on the Aloha Tower alone.

"Children can be selfish—even the adult ones. Clueless, too," Betty said. "But it worked out for the best because we met one another."

She smiled broadly.

Caroline returned her smile. "We sure did, and it was a nice surprise. But what about you? Are you married?"

"I was. Fifty-three years and he's been gone now for a long time. He used to take these cruises with me, and before he died, he made me promise that I'd keep doing them for as long as I enjoyed it. He didn't want me to just sit around the house and mope about being lonely."

Caroline nearly cringed. It sounded like a description of herself.

"That's really nice, but this cruise was a splurge for us, and I can't see myself doing another in the future. We come from modest means, and we spent most of our money on three college educations and just getting by. I'm comfortable now, but this will probably be a one-time thing for me."

"How truly generous of you to pay for college for your kids," Betty exclaimed. "That's quite a gift and these days, not always the case. So many young adults are saddled with college tuition well into their thirties and longer. I'm sure they are grateful for the debt-free boost into adulthood."

Caroline shrugged. "Not sure if they see it that way. Only one of them is even in a job that is remotely applicable to her degree. She works in a bank. My oldest got a teaching degree but she's a real estate agent. And my youngest stumbled through her four years and came out with a degree in the arts. She still hasn't figured out what she wants to do."

"Wouldn't it be great if life was so cut and dried that you knew exactly what path to follow and stuck to where it led, without getting off course?" Betty said. "But we all know it doesn't work that way. We must find our way and it's never a straight shot."

The silence settled around them for a moment.

"So how do you like the cruise so far?" Betty asked, breaking the solemn moment.

"It's fine. I just wish that James was here to enjoy it with me."

"I get that. My husband was always the most thrilled about our cruises and felt like he was somewhat of a cruise connoisseur."

Caroline smiled.

"But he wasn't always a seasoned traveler," Betty said. "I remember on our first cruise we were out to dinner with our friends on the very last night when I realized we hadn't set our suitcases outside the cabin yet and were going to miss the deadline. This was a long time ago, before they implemented self-embark days. We weren't quite ready to end the evening, so he told me to stay put and he'd go do it and come back. Well, he did and when we finally went in for the night, it was late and I was tipsy, and the suitcases were gone. He was proud of himself that he'd done a good job. The next morning, I got up and saw that all our clothes were still in the drawers and the closet! He'd done exactly as I told him and hadn't thought to actually pack the luggage before setting it out. We had to do the walk of shame off the ship with all our things in clear plastic garbage bags, looking like two roadside tramps."

They were still laughing when Tom returned to the table.

"And here we have your asparagus salad," he said, setting the platters down with a flourish. "I'll have your scallops in coconut vinaigrette sauce out in just a minute or two."

"Thank you," they both said.

Tom treated them as though they were celebrities instead of two old ladies and Caroline blushed.

"He's dreamy," Betty said. "If I were just a few years younger…"

Caroline laughed. Betty was turning out to be a lot of fun.

After they'd left the palace, they'd seen the Mission House that was the oldest standing structure on the island and talked about how the King gave permission for it to be built as a residence for the first company of New England Protestant missionaries. The precut lumber for it was shipped in from Boston, traveling all the way around Cape Horn and arriving on Christmas Day of 1820.

Then they'd strolled through a park that was named after Dr. Sun Yat-sen. Betty told her it was called the Chinatown Gateway Park before it was rededicated to the man who many considered the Father of Modern Day China. He was a founder of the very first revolutionary organization and was integral in organizing the overthrow of the Manchu Dynasty and establishing the Republic of China.

Sadly, along with a few tourist groups and a couple who looked like they were on a romantic tryst in the park, there were nearly a dozen or so homeless people roaming around.

"This salad is amazing," Caroline said. She hadn't realized how hungry she really was until the first bite went in.

"Just wait until the main course."

While they ate their salad, Betty entertained Caroline with more stories of other cruises she'd taken, including her one luxury cruise on a megaship.

"The engines were the size of small buildings, and that's no exaggeration," she said. "The food—well, it was beyond belief. The service was the best I've ever experienced, and the ship was so clean and white it looked like it just slid off the conveyor belt. It was really a splurge and was for our twenty-fifth wedding anniversary. That's when we got the cruise bug, though we could never afford another like that one."

"It sounds really special," Caroline said.

"Oh, it was. We stayed up late every evening because we didn't want to miss a single minute of it. There was one night that we danced together in a secluded corner of one of the decks. The music floated up and my husband said the stars twinkled just for us. I'll never forget that moment."

Caroline didn't know how Betty could talk about such a sentimental memory without breaking down. She wouldn't dare trust herself to do the same, even if she could come up with one that would compete.

"My husband would kick himself in the grave if he knew that now the cruise lines are coming out with things like sea water lap pools for open water swimming, complete with docking ports for kayaks. And beds by the pool decks so guests can sleep under the stars if they prefer. I mean, what will they think of next?"

"I'm sure you'd have to be pretty wealthy to afford to buy a cabin," Caroline said.

"Agreed. It's not something I'll be looking into. So, what did you do before you retired?" Betty asked.

"I was an elementary school teacher. Well, after my girls left home, anyway. Until then I didn't work outside the house. I was the catchall: housekeeper, cook, taxi driver, and even therapist. You know how it is. With three daughters, you wouldn't believe how busy it kept me. It also prepared me well for entering the school system. I had a ton of patience built in by the time I got my degree, and I was ready to work."

"Oh, you went to school later in life?"

Caroline nodded. "Yes. My youngest was in high school and the other two in college when I realized I was going to be left twiddling my thumbs. So, I went back to school. I really enjoyed it, though I tended to be the oldest student in every class."

"That's quite impressive."

"Thank you. What did you do?"

Betty smiled. "Can you guess?"

"Hmm. You were sure a good tour guide!"

They laughed.

"Nope. Though I probably would've enjoyed it more than my real vocation. I was an attorney, specializing in family law. Adoption, divorce, custody battles. All that stuff. It could get daunting, and I retired early."

"It sounds exciting, though," Caroline said.

"It was, at least for the first decade or so. I gave it my

all. More than my all, actually. I gave it too much of my life. It's an easy career to let consume you."

Tom returned with the scallops and asked if there was anything else he could get them.

"What do you think of sharing a bottle of wine?" Betty said, winking at Caroline.

"Well, I don't really drink, but I'm not opposed to it, I suppose."

"Done. Tom, please bring us the house white so we can toast to our new friendship."

He nodded and quietly retreated.

The scallops were just as divine as Betty described and before they knew it, they were gone, and the two of them were sopping up the sauce with bits of bread. It was too delicious to waste.

Tom soon showed up with a bottle of wine and made a production of opening it and pouring it into two crystal glasses. Caroline had never felt so fancy and thought that if James could see her now, he'd be nodding his head in approval. He had always told her she deserved to splurge, but she had been stubborn and sought to maintain her practicality. She'd never wanted to look like she was trying to be fancy.

Tom returned with their main courses, and they were so beautifully plated they looked like art and Caroline was almost afraid to touch hers. Betty started though, and she followed. The steak just about melted in Caroline's mouth, and she wasn't one for Asian dishes, but the beef lotus was surprisingly good, too. She'd never even heard of truffled corn and found it delicious, as well as the fried King mushrooms and pickled garlic. Peggy would be proud of her for eating so well.

Tom cleared the plates. "What about dessert, ladies? Can I interest you in a slice of our divine German honey cake?"

Betty raised her eyebrows at Caroline, questioning.

"I can't," Caroline said. "Really. I cannot eat another bite. This was the best meal I've had in ages, but I'm full."

"Wrap it to go, in two separate containers, Tom," Betty said.

"Absolutely," he said, then twirled and left the table.

Betty distributed the rest of the wine evenly between them.

"I can't believe we drank that whole bottle," Caroline said. "It's going to be an interesting walk back to the ship."

Betty waved her hand in the air. "Oh, don't worry about that. I've already asked Tom to make sure we have a taxi waiting. Let's just enjoy the last of the wine."

Caroline felt relieved. Not only did her feet hurt, but she was really feeling the alcohol. Suddenly she was much happier than she'd been since the trip started. But she could just see herself staggering along the boardwalk, trying to keep up with Betty, who appeared to still have the energy of a twenty-year-old.

"I'm sorry we didn't get to tour Pearl Harbor," Betty said. "Have you already seen it?"

Caroline shook her head. "No, the girls weren't interested in seeing it, so I wasn't going to push the subject.

But if James had made it, that would've been our first stop. He was very interested in history."

"Did he ever talk about Ford Island?"

"I don't think so. Is that near here?"

"Yes, it's an islet in the center of Pearl Harbor. That's where the bulk of the US Navy's Pacific Fleet was anchored when the Japanese Forces attacked the battleships and patrol planes. My eldest brother, Kevin, was a crewman for the Navy on the *USS Arizona*. That morning he and five others were on a platform above the bridge when an explosion hit and blocked their access to evacuate. They were all badly burned and saw only one option to escape, and that was to jump to the water eighty feet below, which was engulfed in fire."

Caroline's mood shifted down a few notches immediately as she held her breath, waiting for Betty to finish the story. No one could survive a drop like that, especially into a kettle of flames.

"They were granted a miracle by a man named Joe George who was on the *USS Vestal* that was moored alongside the *Arizona*. He saw them and disobeying his commander's orders, he threw them a line. Kevin secured the line to the *Arizona* and the six of them used it, climbing hand over hand to the *Vestal* to escape, even still under fire from the Japanese and with the oil burning in high temperatures below them. My brother said it was like climbing over the pits of hell."

"He sounds like a strong man," Caroline said. "A fighter."

"Yes, he definitely had to fight to survive. Two of the men died later that day from their injuries and my brother spent a year recovering in the hospital before he could come home to Maui," Betty said.

She took a long sip of her wine, looking lost in her thoughts for a moment.

"Did he ever go back to the service?" Caroline asked.

"No. His injuries were too debilitating. And the event was something he never got over. They lost over four hundred crew members that day. Up until that time Kevin had written letters back home talking about the grand time he was having. He would tell us the most interesting things, like all about the boxing matches he went to on his Friday nights off, and the Battle of the Bands competitions on Saturday nights. He was really into the swing dancing back then. Actually, just the night before the attack he'd gone to a dance hall and won a jitterbug contest with a partner he'd picked out of the crowd who he didn't even know. He had hoped to meet her again at the next dance and get her name, but he never saw her again after that."

"He stayed in Maui?"

Betty nodded. "Yes, Kevin lived a quiet life in a cottage next to my parents. He became a fisherman for some of the smaller, local eating shops. He married a girl he'd gone to school with, and they had a couple of children who moved to the mainland once they grew up. Unfortunately, Kevin died too young. He had complications from his injuries that would crop up sometimes, and during one flare, infection set in, and they lost him to sepsis at only sixty years old. His wife died about five years later from breast cancer, but I think she could've survived it if she'd have wanted to. I feel like she was ready to go meet my brother."

Caroline could certainly understand that. She'd found herself praying for an early death several times since James' departure.

"Was he your last living relative?" she asked.

"Oh no. I still have a few siblings left on Maui, as well as more than a dozen nieces and nephews. An aunt and uncle or two. We're a big family."

Caroline noticed she didn't mention children of her own and wasn't sure if she should ask. It was a sensitive subject for some.

"Can I ask, how long you've been widowed?" Betty said.

"Four months, three weeks, and five days."

"Oh honey, I'm so sorry. Do you want to talk about it?"

"I'm not sure what I'd say," Caroline said softly. "My world has been rocked. James was the first person I wanted to tell good news, bad news, or really anything to. He helped me get through the drama our adult daughters are always embroiled in. I feel so alone. I mean, I do have two cats and I have no intention of getting more and becoming that kind of old lady."

She tried to smile.

Betty reached over and put her hand on Caroline's. "I get it. I remember the first time I was asked to fill out an emergency contact at the doctor's office. I had to find their restroom and hide there until I could breathe again through the sobbing. And the business part of all of it. Wow—so much to change. I had a meltdown when my credit cards were cancelled because even though my name was on them, my husband had opened the accounts and simply added me as an authorized user. We had an excellent rating on all of them, but I was forced to start from scratch and apply for my own."

"Oh no. I haven't heard anything from ours. I guess I should check on that," Caroline said.

"If you try to use them, they'll let you know really fast. But I guess what I wanted to say to you is that it will get easier. It's a cliché but time really does help. You'll find your stride, but it may take a while. Be kind to yourself in the meantime."

Caroline didn't know how to do that. She felt like such a failure without James. She felt useless and used up and didn't see how it would ever improve.

She looked out the window and saw that the sky was beginning to pinken.

"Oh no, we need to get back to the meeting place," she exclaimed, looking at her watch. Then she pulled her phone from her bag and saw she had seven missed calls from the girls, and more than a dozen text messages. She'd forgotten to turn her audio back on after Tabby's speech at the Tower.

The girls would be livid and think she had purposely ignored them. Suddenly she felt like a schoolgirl who had stayed out past curfew.

Betty put her hand in the air to motion to Tom and he rushed over and took her card.

"I can't thank you enough for today," Caroline said. "I'm truly overwhelmed with your kindness. Can I at least leave the tip?"

"No, thank you. The gratuity will be added to the card. I'm so grateful for your company, Caroline, so consider us even," Betty said. "And this isn't the last of us. We still have a few days on the ship to get to know each other. I hope I'll get to meet your daughters."

Caroline nodded in agreement. Silently, she hoped they'd behave.

Five

They were up for early breakfast, and it was going to be a quiet one. All the girls were there, but the ship had veered into bad weather during the night and the high winds and heaving sea had been rough on everyone.

"Mom, I need more coffee," Rachel said from behind her dark sunglasses. She still looked pale.

Instead of waiting for someone to come around with a refill, Caroline rose and took Rachel's cup to where she'd seen the drinks set up. She refilled the cup and returned, then set it down in front of her youngest and currently most needy child.

"We paid a lot of money for this cruise. You'd think they would have a way of controlling the pitch of the boat," Peggy said as she dumped a small cup of blueberries into her oatmeal.

"Right," Laura replied. "Because if you pay enough money, they can call Mother Nature and reserve a calm voyage. Great tip."

"You know what I mean," Peggy said.

"Girls, please. We got through it and the sun is up, so let's try to be optimistic," Caroline chided. If anyone should be grumpy, it should be her. She was the one who'd spent the entire night taking care of someone else. She'd held Rachel's hair back while she vomited, and even kept a cool cloth on her head for the most part. She'd sucked up her own seasickness to take care of her child—a grown child, at that—because that's what mothers do, no matter how old their kids were.

And whether their children were grateful or not.

"You aren't off the hook, yet, Mom," Peggy said, directing her ire at Caroline. "You had us worried to death. What were you thinking by not answering your calls or messages yesterday?"

"First, I've already apologized. I forgot that while Tabby the cat leader was talking, I'd turned my sound off. And second, I didn't miss the meetup time established by her, and I made it back to the ship by last call, so you really had no reason to be alarmed. I'm here, aren't I? Not tucked away in the arms of some kidnapper or in the trunk of his car. I already told you I was with my new friend, Betty."

Peggy and Laura exchanged their first morning eye roll.

"You have to do better, Mom. What if we'd have called the police?" Laura said. "That would've been embarrassing. And you never know, this Betty-person might be someone trying to scam you out of money. Have you thought of that?"

Caroline was saved from answering.

"Good morning," Betty said as she approached the table carrying a plate of fruit and a cup of orange juice. Today she was dressed in turquoise and purple tones, somewhat like a peacock, but in fabrics that looked svelte and expensive.

"Good morning, Betty. Please, sit down." Caroline gestured at an empty chair.

The two oldest girls immediately sat up straighter, curious now to see what Betty looked like.

Rachel didn't budge. She was still a bit green.

"The girls are a bit under the weather from last night, but let me introduce them to you," Caroline said. When she was through making the introductions, she breathed a sigh of relief that the girls were polite in their greetings. She had, after all, raised them that way but considering their moods, they had her worried for a minute.

"It's nice to meet all of you. Sorry to hear that you had a rough night. I hope you at least got a chance to go out on the deck and wish upon a star before those mean clouds rolled in last night," Betty said.

"We all did," Rachel said. "But Mom goes to bed too early for that. I'm sure she's made plenty of wishes over the years, though."

Hmm, they'd wished on stars without her. Caroline hadn't known that.

Betty looked dismayed for a moment but recovered quickly. "Well, thank you for letting me borrow her yesterday. She made for a great port partner, and we had just the best time!"

"So, you're with the cat group, too?" Peggy asked.

"Oh no. I'm cruising alone. That's why it was so

wonderful for me to run into your mom at the top of the Aloha Tower. Both of us were on our own, so we decided to be on our own together."

"You weren't with the group, Mom?" Rachel asked.

"I was, but then I went to the top of the tower, and I met Betty." Caroline wasn't about to tell them that she had no plans of walking around with the cat group.

"Where did you two go?" Laura asked, her tone suspicious.

Caroline put aside the fact that the girls hadn't asked her a thing about her day when they'd come to her cabin last night. They were full of telling her about all the wonderful things they'd done and seen and had showed no interest in anything else.

"We started out at a palace, if you can imagine that," Caroline said, then filled them in on the highlights. Betty broke in a few times when describing the special steak and how well Tom took care of them.

"I'm so jealous of the meal," Laura said. "We ate bar food."

"Sounds fun, Mom," Peggy said. "But good ol' Tom might not be so nice if he didn't think you were two rich old ladies about to drop a big tip on him."

Silence fell around the table. Caroline was mortified.

"Wow, Peggy," Rachel said. "Can you be any more of an ass?"

Thankfully her daughter had the courtesy to blush.

Betty laughed. "It's okay. She's right and I'm aware of the fact that at fancy restaurants, the staff might think a little schmoozing will get them some green love. I'd do the same in their shoes! But Tom really was a kind soul, too. I could tell."

"I agree," Caroline said. She shot Peggy a look. She'd deal with her later.

"Well, I wish we could get your Tom on deck to take care of some customer service in our cabin," Laura said.

"What's wrong?" Caroline asked.

Laura sighed. "You mean aside from the way our air conditioner hisses through the vent over our beds and sounds like a dragon coming through? Then we finally figured out we could turn off the speaker that pipes music in, but we have no control over the obnoxiously loud hallway intercom system. It also takes forever for the hot water to start coming through for a shower, which by the way, was made for Snow White's seven dwarves, judging by the size of it."

"Jeez, Laura," Rachel said. "Want some cheese with that whine? You have your own bed, don't you?"

"Laura's right," Peggy said. "Can I also add that the midnight buffet sucks to high heaven? They cook all the nutrients out of their vegetables and don't get me started on the quality of their fruit. I hope while we're in Maui they'll be picking up some fresh supplies for the route back."

"Well, I think the food is just fine," Rachel said. "Since when were you two born with a silver spoon up your butts? Also, you told me you'd text me if you were going to do the midnight buffet. I knew I'd miss out on stuff because I'm not in the same room."

Caroline cringed, and she knew she needed to stop

the crying train. "I think you girls are a bit homesick and missing your kids."

"Don't make excuses for them, Mom," Rachel said, as though she were a perfect angel.

"I'm sorry everything isn't to your liking," Betty said. "But you must admit, the ship offers a lot in the way of activities. You've got a lot to choose from. I've already done the lei-making class twice and I'm thinking of learning to dance the hula before this trip is over. What about all of you?"

"If you do the lei class again, I might try that," Caroline said. "I don't see myself learning to rotate my hips. These hips have hung up their right to sway."

Betty laughed. "Fair enough, and I'll be glad to accompany you to the lei-making. To be honest, I had to show the instructor a few things myself. A delightful young girl, but I think she's new."

"We went to the production of *Grease*, and it was great," Peggy said.

"Oh? I was there, too! I loved it. Sometimes the cruise shows are a hit or a miss but that one is well done. I was on a cruise once when they had a British hypnotist. You should've seen what he did to his volunteers."

"I don't believe in hypnotists," Peggy said.

"I do," Rachel said. "I had a friend a few years ago who was training to perform hypnosis on moms in labor and she wanted me to be her guinea pig. I wasn't pregnant, by the way. But it was a relaxing experience and I enjoyed it. What did the cruise hypnotist make them do?"

Betty laughed. "One of the ladies on stage believed

her seat was heating up like fire and kept hopping up and down from it. A man was taken back to his childhood and thought the lady next to him was his mommy and continually told her he needed to wee-wee."

They all laughed.

"Then a few of them kept strutting around the stage waving their arms because they thought they were flamingos taking flight," Betty said. "He told one lady that she was a rock star drum player and you should've seen her banging her imaginary drums!"

"That's just amazing to me," Caroline said. "I'm glad there's not one on board here because I think it's scary that someone has that kind of power over your mind."

"It was interesting, to be sure," Betty said.

"Actually, I've read up on hypnosis before and scientific research supports evidence that hypnosis can be used to treat a lot of conditions like chronic pain and depression," Laura said.

"And phobias and anxiety," Rachel added.

"So, what do you do in real life, Betty? Considering you take so many cruises, I'm curious," Peggy said, looking down her nose at Betty like a jaguar waiting to pounce. "Or is that top secret?"

"A secret? How did you know?" Betty said, her expression serious as a heart attack. "To be honest, I just got out of prison."

Caroline just about fell out of her chair.

"But I can tell you what I did in prison. My job was lead caretaker of the bathroom on our quad. There was always a contest to see which section had the cleanest and

I knew the secret to getting us that trophy. Want to know what it was?"

No one said a word. Even Rachel had lowered her sunglasses to get a better look at Betty.

"Ketchup!" Betty said. "Ketchup has vinegar in it and gives metal a shine you wouldn't believe. We'd all grab our allowed one packet at chow time and save it, then I'd disburse it to my cleaning buddies, and we'd make sure the job got done right. The tiles and grout were harder to clean but when I put that shine on the faucets and handles, that's what the eyes were drawn to and got us a win every time. I'm sure the girls are sad I got early release but hopefully someone is still using my secret formula."

Betty gave Caroline a wink when she finished, but Rachel saw it.

"You're kidding, right?" she asked.

Caroline couldn't help but laugh, and Betty joined in. The girls didn't think it was so funny and simply stared at them like they'd lost their minds.

"Oh—oh—" Betty tried to talk between breaths. "I'm sorry. I couldn't help myself."

"She wasn't in prison," Caroline said, finally able to control her own laughter.

"But I was an attorney! Close enough, right? Except I did family law."

"I know plenty of attorneys in prison. Make the right mistake and boom," Peggy said, no trace of humor present. "You're writing letters for felons and creating motions for a pouch of noodles."

"Oh honey," Betty said. "I've learned so much from

my mistakes. I'm thinking of making a few more, but so far it's nothing that would land me in jail. So anyway, what are you all planning to do for your first Maui day?"

"I hired a car and driver to take us on the Road to Hana tour," Peggy said. "But we're splitting the cost."

Rachel sat back in her chair and groaned. "Yes, Peggy. For the fifteenth time, we are splitting the cost. You don't have to keep saying it. I'll send you my part on cash app."

"Have you all tried the omelet station on the upper stern deck?" Betty asked, expertly deflecting the conversation to something else. "It's so much better than the eggs you can get on the buffet. It's quiet up there, too, and it's not so cold in the mornings."

"Great tip. I'll try that tomorrow," said Caroline.

"Let me know if you all need any help with your Maui plans for today or tomorrow. I'm assuming you'll be spending the night on the ship and not getting a hotel?" Betty asked around the table.

"I wanted to get a hotel for the night since it's a two-day port, but no one else wanted to spend the money," Peggy said. "Why? Are you getting a special deal we need to know of?"

"No, not really. But I know just about all the business owners and can tell you which ones to trust," Betty said.

"Betty is from Maui," Caroline explained. "She still has family here. But she lives in California now."

"Oh, wow. That must be nice to come visit and not have to pay the steep hotel prices," Laura said.

"Why don't you just live here?" Rachel asked.

"It's nice to have a place to stay if I want, and the

reason I don't live here is because after I went to college, it was easier to find a job on the mainland. Then I met my husband, and we put down roots where we were. We preferred the busier city life over the slow pace of Maui."

"I can't imagine not wanting to live on an island if I could," Rachel said. "To have nice weather all the time and be able to swim or surf when you please. It would be paradise."

"I'm sure like any town, Maui has its disadvantages to the locals," Caroline said.

Betty nodded. "It sure does now. Back when I was a child, the town wasn't a tourist magnet yet. It wasn't crowded and driving from one end to the other wasn't the nightmare it is now."

"We hired a driver for today," Peggy cut in. "His name is Richard and he's going to take us to Hana."

"Richard Cano?" Betty asked.

"Yes, that's it."

"Oh, he's great. He'll make sure you see what's important and skip the overcrowded sites. I'm so glad you all aren't doing the organized shore excursions. You did good."

"Thank you," Peggy said, beaming from the praise.

"Ask him to take you by Paia Fish Market or Hula Grill on the way back for some lunch. And Nectar Creations is a great boutique for gifts and souvenirs," Betty added. "I'm glad you aren't sticking to just touring Lahaina Front Street. It's so packed it's hard to get around when the cruise ships come in. Though if you get the chance when you're coming back, you might want to see the old Banyan Tree in front of the courthouse. It's been growing there since 1873 and has seen a lot of history under its sprawling branches."

"Oh, I'd like to see that," Caroline said.

"It's quite a wonder," Betty said. "The original tree is more than sixty feet high, and its limbs stretch out like an octopus for the distance of a city block. It was only eight feet tall when it was planted at the order of Queen Keōpūolani to commemorate the fiftieth anniversary of the first American Protestant mission in Lahaina."

Rachel said. "I want to get some pictures so I can sketch it later."

"Just beware, you'll see some lost souls wandering around and about there, and they might ask you for a dollar or some change, but they're usually harmless," Betty said.

"No worries. I'm a bit of a lost soul myself sometimes." Rachel lifted her sunglasses and peeked at her phone, then stood abruptly. "Oh, shoot. We need to get back to the room and get our stuff. It's just about time to disembark."

"I came ready," Peggy said, patting her beach bag confidently.

Rachel looked at her sisters. "Oh, I have those patches in my bag if you want to come by and get one. I read the roads are pretty twisty going up to Hana and they'll help with carsickness."

"I could've used that last night with the way the ship was listing," Laura said.

"Seriously," Peggy agreed. She stood to join Laura. "Thanks for letting us know, *Rachel*."

The sarcasm wasn't lost on their little sister. "Sorry.

Once I started heaving, I couldn't think of anything else but getting through it. Besides, I would've thought you'd have your own, Peggy. You are usually the best-prepared."

"Mom, are you coming?" Laura asked. "You need to get your stuff."

"I'll be along in a minute."

The girls said their goodbyes to Betty, a polite gesture that made Caroline proud. Once they'd left the table, she looked at Betty.

"I just want to know one thing," she said.

"Shoot," Betty replied.

"Does ketchup really make the faucets sparkle?"

They both laughed until they were wiping tears away.

Caroline finally found the right hallway after getting her bearings and she picked up the pace. The girls would be fussing at her for taking too long, but she had been preoccupied after leaving Betty and why did all the hallways have to look the same on a cruise ship anyway?

As she approached the cabin, she could hear their voices behind the door. She had no plans to eavesdrop but before she could get her key card out of her pocket, she heard Peggy.

"I'll get her to understand that she has to move right now while it's a seller's market and she can get the best price. If she waits too long, the bubble is going to pop, and the house will go down in value."

Caroline felt sick at her stomach, even though she

wasn't surprised. This was exactly what she'd feared the girls were up to.

"I brought some brochures from the senior living place that I liked best," Laura said. "The one that has the best list of activities. The only issue is that she won't be able to bring those cats."

"Wait—we can't make her get rid of Felix and Fauci. Dad loved those boys," Rachel said.

Caroline wanted to cheer for Rachel. Maybe her youngest would be her ally.

"But maybe we can find them a home together," Rachel added. "I know a girl who works in cat rescue. How old are they, anyway?"

So much for Rachel sticking up for her.

"We just need to get through today and at dinner tonight, we'll talk about everything," Peggy said. "From what I read, some of the best stops take quite a hike to see the good stuff. Like Black Sand Beach and the Seven Pools. Mom won't be able to do those, so we'll have to skip them. But maybe she'll want to stay on board tomorrow and we can hit those."

"Then why don't we just do Front Street so we could shop while she sits on a bench or something?" Rachel said. "There's an art gallery there I would love to see."

"We've already planned the day so let's stick to it. If she'd hurry up, that is. I want to be in the first group to disembark so we don't get caught up behind the slow old folks," Laura said.

Slow old folks?

Caroline couldn't feel more disappointed in her daughters than she did at that moment. Not only for their callous depiction of *old folks*, but for their scheming behind her back. It wasn't like she was senile or couldn't think for herself. Heck, she wasn't even that old yet!

What hurt the most is they weren't the least bit excited about making memories with her on Maui. She was a hindrance to them, it appeared. A chain around their ankle.

She used her key card and went in.

"There you are," Laura said. "What took so long?"

"Mom, you're going to make us late for Richard," Peggy said. She looked at Caroline as though she were a disobedient toddler.

Caroline sat down on the bed. "I had to stop at the bathroom. Not feeling too well."

"Oh no, was it the breakfast?" Peggy asked. "I told you the food here is not healthy."

"The food is fine, or I'd be sick, too," Rachel said. "We ate the same thing."

Laura nodded in agreement.

"I think I'm just worn out," Caroline lied. "Why don't you girls take the day to yourselves, and I'll stay on board and enjoy the peace and quiet? I have a book I've been wanting to dig into. I'm looking forward to it, actually."

They looked at each other, unsure what to do.

"Well, maybe you should go to the medical office?" Rachel said. "Do you have a fever?"

Caroline shook her head. "No, I'm sure I'll be fine later. I just want to be alone today."

"Mom, are you wallowing?" Peggy asked. "We can't

let you keep being so sad. That's why we're on this cruise. To help you get over losing Dad."

Caroline felt her irritation rise to the top. "What makes you think that taking a cruise will lift the weight of my grief and make it magically float away?"

Peggy looked taken aback.

"I don't think that's what she meant, Mom," Laura said.

"Well, that's what it feels like to me," Caroline said, hearing the bite in her tone but unable to keep it out. "What you girls don't realize is this isn't an alternate reality just because you got me away from home. My sorrow is circling this ship like the pale blue dorsal fin of a great white, just waiting on me to step back into real life. It's no use running from it, and I want you to give me the time I need. Just go and I'll be fine here today. Really."

She didn't mean to sound so sharp, but they were lucky she didn't blast them about the plans they were making for her life. She needed time to think about how to react when they finally brought up their idea about the house; have her ducks in a row so she would sound like she knew what she was saying. She sure didn't want to give them more reason to think she needed to be coddled.

"Maybe we should all just stay on board today," Laura said.

"No," Rachel replied. "I think we should respect Mom's wishes that she wants to be alone."

"I agree," Peggy said.

"Great. Have fun, girls," Caroline said, then went

into the small bathroom and shut the door. Being alone was the last thing she wanted. But what was worse than being alone was being unwanted.

A half hour later, Caroline found a place on one of the upper decks and leaned on the banister, watching guests disembark. She hadn't seen the girls go by yet and guessed they were being held up by Peggy either on her phone or checking her email.

She made sure she was tucked away enough that they wouldn't see her and have second thoughts. Even if they begged her to come, at this point she would still stay no.

All around her was an air of excitement, so many people thrilled for their chance to get off the boat and experience Maui. For some it was a dream that was years in the making, just like it would have been for James.

Caroline couldn't shake the sadness. Not for herself—she was tough, and she'd get through all the mess eventually and didn't want any pity—but for James, and the things he didn't get to do or see.

She really did have several new books saved on her e-reader, but the truth was, she just couldn't concentrate enough to get into any of them. She wasn't that interested in laying by the pool, either because she sure didn't need any more sun and even if she did, she didn't relish having to pass by the hairy-stomach guy who so far on the cruise seemed to be there no matter what time they happened to go by the pool. He didn't take a chaise. No

—he sat in one of the upright chairs you had to pass to get to the pool.

With her luck, he was staying on board as well. God forbid he'd think she was lonely and break his trance to start up a conversation.

"Caroline? What are you doing up here?"

She turned to find Betty.

"Oh, I'm just watching. James used to tell me that I had more fun people-watching than any other kind of activity he could tempt me with."

"Me, too. But where are your girls? Shouldn't you be in line to get off the ship?" Betty asked. She herself looked ready to disembark, the straps of two full cloth bags over her arms.

Caroline shrugged. "I told them to go on without me today. I think I'll have a poolside day. Catch up on my reading."

She was lying, and they both knew it.

Betty narrowed her eyes at Caroline and set her bags down. "What's going on? There's something you aren't telling me. Spit it out."

"No, not at all," Caroline said, shaking her head. "I just think they don't need their old mother trailing along and holding them up. They want to get out and hike to the waterfalls, go through the bamboo forest, and all sorts of adventurous things. I want them to really get their money's worth today. They can't do all that if I'm with them."

"Well, if you ask me, that's just ridiculous. There's lots of ways to enjoy Maui without being a triathlete."

"It's fine, Betty. Really," Caroline said, embarrassed now.

"No, it's not. What is fine, though, is that I happened to see you standing here because otherwise you might miss the opportunity of a lifetime."

"What opportunity?"

"The opportunity to spend a day with a Maui native," Betty said. "Go get your stuff, ol' girl. You're coming with me."

Caroline started to object but before she could get one word out, Betty held her hand up.

"Go. Get. Your. Stuff."

"What do I need?" she asked, giving up. Betty wasn't going to take no for an answer.

"Whatever you would've taken had you gone with the girls. Don't forget your swimsuit, too. I'll wait right here and if you don't come back in fifteen minutes, I'll come find you."

Caroline fully believed she would, so she hurried along.

Six

Caroline sat in the backseat and chuckled to herself, still feeling silly from the scene that she and Betty had made getting off the ship. Instead of waiting in the long line to disembark, Betty had slid on some dark sunglasses, grabbed Caroline's arm for an escort, and pretended to be blind. Her trick had worked, and the crowd had let them by, as though Moses himself was parting the Red Sea.

"You don't stop laughing when you get old, you get old when you stop laughing," Betty said as they made their way to the parking lot and found her sister standing beside a black Ford Taurus.

"You made it!"

The two of them embraced and rocked back and forth for a moment before separating.

"And who do we have here?" her sister asked, then gave Caroline a quick embrace, too.

Betty took the dark glasses off and made introductions. Caroline could see the resemblance that made it impossible to think of them as anything but sisters.

In the front seat, Betty and her sister chatted back and forth, and Caroline noticed how easily they got along, catching up on family news and what was happening in each other's lives and on the island. It gave her hope that one day, her own girls could have such an easy relationship.

Betty turned her head toward the back. "Are you cool enough back there?"

"Yes, I'm fine." Caroline felt a bit awkward after Betty had explained to her sister that they'd met on the ship and decided to spend the day together.

"Caroline is from Colorado, so she's not used to such hot and humid temperatures," Betty said to her sister, Gracie, who had picked them up at the port.

"Oh, how nice. I've always wanted to see the mountains there," Gracie said.

"They are indeed beautiful," Caroline said. "My husband loved to ski when he was younger. He taught all of our daughters."

Physically, it was obvious that Betty and Gracie were sisters, but Gracie's features showed more of their Chinese background, while Betty's Hawaiian heritage seemed to show through more. Gracie wore a billowy white shirt over a colorful Hawaiian sarong, her tiny feet slipped into sandals, looking very comfortable and unencumbered.

They were both very lovely, having aged gracefully and seemed comfortable in their own skins.

Caroline wished that she could feel the same. Her skin felt clunky. And old.

Within a few minutes, they pulled up to a small two-story clapboard home that boasted an inviting porch with colorful chimes hanging from the eaves in several places.

"We're here," Gracie said as she cut off the motor.

"We'll freshen up and then decide what to do with the day," Betty said to Caroline. "I usually just hang around with family—and eat, of course—but with this being your first time to Maui, we'll go out and about and look around."

"You could take her shopping at the Maui Swap Meet, or even the Upcountry Farmer's Market," Gracie said. "Though that would be quite a drive."

"I was thinking maybe the Maui's Farmers and Crafters market," Betty said. "I haven't stopped in there for ages, and I'd like her to see something off the tourist track."

"Oh no," Caroline said. "Please, don't change your plans because of me. I'm fine with whatever we do and anyway, my feet might not be up for too much walking."

"Don't try to talk her out of it," Gracie said, winking at Caroline. "Betty loves to be a tour guide on the island, and she'll show you all the good stuff."

"She did just that on Honolulu," Caroline said. "We had the best time."

"We sure did," Betty said. "And we will again today. Come on, let's go on in."

Caroline noticed the Chinese characters carved into the wooden shutters as she passed by. The chimes from the porch created a lyrical song with the slight wind that blew through, a silent welcoming to what felt like was going to be a cozy place to get her bearings.

Both Betty and Gracie slipped off their shoes at the front door, so Caroline did the same.

Inside, they went through a small front living room that looked comfortable but elegant with a red velvet sofa and matching chairs, a beautiful seascape painting on the wall.

Betty led the way upstairs to a small bedroom.

"You can leave your stuff in here, and the bathroom is just over there," she gestured down the hall. "Take your time. I'll use Gracie's room. Put your swimsuit on if you think you'll want to get wet somewhere."

When she left, Caroline sat down on the chair in the corner of the room. She pulled her phone from her bag and checked it.

Nothing yet. She hoped the girls had found their driver.

She put her phone away.

There wasn't much freshening up needed, as they hadn't done anything yet, but Caroline took her bag to the bathroom and stood in front of the mirror.

Unlike the Maui sisters, her aging face wasn't as pleasing. Below the neck was even worse, and there was no way she was going to be putting on a swimsuit. Her cropped pants were cool to wear and covered enough of her not to scare anyone.

She applied her sunscreen, some protective lip balm, then tucked it all away and went downstairs, following the sound of laughter to the kitchen.

"Caroline, grab a seat," Betty said, gesturing for her to join them at the table.

"Yes, join us," Gracie said. "You look refreshed already. Do I dare see a summer glow on your face?"

Caroline laughed softly. "I just put on some tinted sunscreen."

"I get my summer glow from a bottle," Betty said. "A bottle of Maui Blanc, that is. I've been wanting this for months. I depleted my own stash at my birthday dinner in February."

They laughed and Betty poured some of the wine in a glass and pushed it toward Caroline.

While she'd been upstairs, they had whipped together a platter of fruit and cheese, and it looked delicious. Caroline felt her stomach rumble and she picked up a piece of cheese and popped it into her mouth.

"This wine is made from Maui Gold pineapples grown right here on the island," Betty said. "I take a few bottles home every time I come to visit."

"That might be something that Caroline wants to visit," Gracie said. "The history there is interesting. Back in the 1850s the building was used as a holding place for prisoners before they were transported to the county jail. The walls are the original lava rock and more than three feet thick."

"Not sure we can do that and manage much else, since it's way up in Kula," Betty said. "But it is interesting. Even before that, the cottage was originally an office for a plantation owner. He started out as a whaling captain, then like others, he turned to ranching and was owner of a huge plantation. It's said that he was most famous for his parties. Lots of drinking and dancing, and even horse racing. He had a cellar in there with a hatch door and when some of the partygoers got out of hand, they were sent down and shackled to the wall until they sobered up."

Caroline laughed. "I suppose that's one way to take care of them."

She took a sip of the wine. It was delicious with a sweet, tropical flavor she'd never experienced in a wine. She could see herself becoming a wine drinker if she had easy access to one as tasty as it was.

"It's so good," she said. "But I'd better not drink too much, or I'll spend the day napping."

"Well, we don't want that," Betty said. "I have a few places I want to show you."

"Gracie, are you coming with us?" Caroline asked.

Gracie shook her head. "No, I'm working on a project for a friend. We're tracing her lineage back to figure out where her family originated from."

"My sister has a knack for research," Betty said. "Some people pay her to trace their families back to a specific person."

"That's fascinating," Caroline said. "Have you always been in that line of work?"

"I've always been interested in history, but I didn't pick this up until I retired and needed to find more to do with my time. Turns out I'm pretty good at it and it gives me purpose, I guess you could say."

"It can be useful in finding missing persons, too," Betty said. "Gracie was involved in a very important case of a missing child from Maui a few years back. She's also been instrumental in helping people find lost loved ones. What they can do these days with DNA is phenomenal."

"That sounds intriguing," Caroline said. She envied Gracie for having a sense of purpose. "I'd love to hear more."

"Maybe tonight at the family get-together," Betty said. "We need to get going now or all you'll have for Maui memories is these four walls."

It sounded just fine to Caroline because the sisters were mesmerizing to listen to, but it would be nice to see a bit of the island, too.

Betty led her out to the car, which Caroline noticed that she didn't even ask her sister to use, it was just assumed it was fine. They got in and Betty turned to her.

"What would you like to see first?"

"Hmm. I really have no idea except it may need to be something that doesn't require a ton of walking."

"Then let's start with Front Street and go from there," Betty said. "I know we saw a bit of it, but I'll drive you by and let you get a good look."

As she drove, Betty talked about Maui and the serious situation of too many people and unaffordable housing since the rich had come in and bought up so many properties.

"What was it like growing up here?" Caroline asked.

"It was as enchanting as you can probably imagine. I feel like I grew up in a cozy bubble of safety. Until I went to college on the mainland, I didn't realize how big the world was because here on the island you could drive around the whole thing in three hours, and that was considered a long road trip."

Caroline laughed.

"I'm serious," Betty said, joining her in laughter. "It was a different kind of life back then. Many of us went to school barefoot and it wasn't looked down upon, it was just expected. We were surrounded by so many different cultures that it wasn't even noticed, and we sure didn't have problems with racism. Not that I remember, anyway. Those were the days when students respected their teachers, and teachers were allowed to discipline the students. We were all terrified of a call to our parents from the principal, and let me tell you, that never happened in my house."

"Now that sounds familiar," Caroline said. "We always had a healthy fear of my parents and teachers, too. It taught us to be respectful."

Betty nodded. "I miss those days when we knew our place and felt safe in it. After school let out, we'd play in the streets or in someone's yard until dark and we ate dinner wherever we were at, as neighbors fed whatever kid was there at the time. Then Saturdays were usually spent helping with chores at home until noon. Boys mowed the grass and helped pick up dropped coconuts. Girls helped with the laundry and babysat. Clothes were hung on the lines outdoors to dry, and yards were colorful with wet swimsuits and towels hanging on the clotheslines."

"Most neighborhoods now won't even allow clotheslines," Caroline said.

Betty turned down a new street. "Right. The dreaded invention of HOAs. We didn't have that back then. Of course, we also didn't even have air-conditioning. All our doors and windows would be left open for the trade winds to come through. Didn't matter how hot it got because we'd all be heading to the ocean in the afternoon to cool off."

"That would be amazing," Caroline said, envisioning a pack of children running for the water and diving in.

"It was," Betty said. "Television wasn't a thing because no one stayed inside if there was any light outside. Sometimes on the weekends we'd all climb into the back of a pickup truck and a parent would take us to find some cliffs to jump from into the water."

"Weren't you scared?" Caroline asked.

"Maybe a little," Betty said. "But it was a rite of passage and once you took a big jump, you were no longer one of the little kids. You instantly moved up to the next group."

"It sounds like a lovely way to grow up."

Betty nodded. "It was. Those were the times that families stayed together. They worshiped together, found a way to make ends meet, and had a sense of pride in the modest way they built their families. Even during the hard times, life was good because we were together, and we'd always find a way to make it work. And in hard times if we needed help, someone would always step in. The islands always shared a strong sense of community that's hard still to find on the mainland."

"Here's the famous Banyan Tree," Betty said, slowing the car to a crawl.

The tree was just as amazing as she'd described it and Caroline could just imagine children using it to hide among the cavernous trunks and beneath the long tresses of moss that hung from the branches. Benches lined the area and there were a few people sitting around.

"Gracie and I used to hunt chameleons in there," Betty said. "I'm sure kids still do that."

"What is the building back there?" Caroline asked, pointing at the building that sat behind the trees.

"It used to be the old customs house and court affairs. They built it with material from one of the palaces that was destroyed during a windstorm before it could be completed. Now there's a museum upstairs and a gallery gift shop on the first floor."

Betty drove around the block. "This is the famous Front Street," she said. "You'll see most of the cruisers here and we can park if you'd like to do any shopping."

Caroline shook her head. "No, that's fine. I'd rather keep sightseeing if you don't mind."

"Not at all," Betty said. "I never get tired of taking in the beauty of Maui. Especially when I've been gone a while."

They drove for a bit, getting a glimpse of the ocean between properties, then Betty pulled off and parked behind a line of cars and shut off the engine. "This is the Napili area and there's a secret beach that only the locals know. It's easy to get to if you'd like to walk down to the water."

"Sure," Caroline agreed.

They climbed out of the car and Betty led the way off the road, past a grove of trees and onto a narrow, worn path.

At the end it opened onto a small beach tucked into the curve of the land.

"You can never tell anyone where this is," Betty said, opening her arms wide as though presenting a show. "We call it Hammock Island."

And a show it was because behind her the sun glinted across the top of the ocean, twinkling into a cascade of shimmering light with each wave. The small strip of beach was secluded, no sign of anyone else, only them and the gentle noise of the waves crashing against the shore.

"It's beautiful," Caroline said, her voice almost silent in an awed hush. She saw a large rock and had a sudden flashback of a memory. "This reminds me of the time that James and I were first married, before kids, and we took a vacation to Canada. We rented a small boat and went out to a small, rocky island and camped. James fished every morning and we played cards at night."

Betty laid a towel on the sand, and they sat.

Caroline stared out at a big rock that was partially submerged in the shallow water. "There was a big rock like that one and one afternoon, we lay on the rock and sunbathed, letting the water softly lap at our feet. It was such a simple and sweet time, before life got complicated. I haven't thought of it for years."

"I'm so glad you shared that with me," Betty said.

"It was a magical moment. That's the only way I can explain it," Caroline replied. She turned to Betty. "Thank you for sharing this spot with me so I could bring that memory back."

A small splash in the water got their attention and they both turned to see a large sea turtle. It raised its head at them, nodded, then submerged again.

"A turtle," Caroline exclaimed excitedly.

"Yes, they pop up now and again here. If you'd like to see more, I can take you up to Ho'okipa Beach near Paia. There's a surfer crowd there as well as a larger beach where dozens of turtles come to rest every day."

"I think I'm happy to see just one," Caroline said. "What I'd really like to do is go sit on that rock for a moment and remember James."

"Then do it, sister! Want me to come with you or would you like to be alone?"

"Whatever you want." Caroline said. She bent down and rolled her pant legs up further.

"I think I'll give you a minute with your memories."

Caroline waded out to the rock and carefully climbed on top of it, then sat and looked out at the ocean. There was so much she wanted to say to James, but suddenly the words left her and all she wanted was to remember his face. The strong, stubborn set of his jaw and the constant stubble that was there, no matter what time he shaved. His deep brown eyes and the way they sparkled when he called her his girl, even when they both knew she was a long way from the girl he'd first known. The way he always embraced life, never letting the aches and pains of old age get him down or squash his joy.

Suddenly she knew she really didn't need to see any more of Maui. They could even go back to the ship, for all she cared.

The view from where she sat, the warm rock, and the sweet memory they both brought her was enough, and quite frankly, a gift she hadn't expected.

She climbed down and began wading back to the beach.

A sparkle in the water caught her eye and she bent to see what it was, thinking it could be a ring, or a pendant.

But no, it was not jewelry.

It was another dime.

They'd had lunch and were cruising along the Pali Highway, looking out over the cliff sides at the ocean scenery. Caroline was full as a tick, and she leaned her head against the car window, feeling suddenly drowsy.

Betty looked over and smiled. "We'll be back at Gracie's in ten minutes, and we can have an afternoon nap," she said. "What did you think about Leoda's Kitchen and Pie Shop? Their tagline is *glorified grandma country food*, though I don't know any grandmothers who are that good in the kitchen!"

"That was absolutely the most amazing pie I've ever had in my life," Caroline said. "The sandwich was great, too, but wow—who knew pie could be that good? All my life I've said I'd rather have cake than pie, and now I'm wondering why."

"Right? The hardest part is deciding which pie to get when I'm there. I usually go with the coconut cream, but today the peanut butter pie called out to me louder. And Gracie is going to be at my beck and call since I brought her favorite Lemonade and Olowalu Lime pie for her."

"I probably should've gotten some to take to the girls," Caroline said. "That banana cream was to die for, and I'd never heard of a Guava Chiffon pie, but it looked good, too. Along with that huge avocado cucumber sandwich, my body feels like it's going into a food coma."

"We've got time if you want to take a nap before I take you back to the ship. Or we can even do a bit more looking around, if you like."

It sounded tempting. Caroline looked at her phone and saw that Laura had texted to ask how she was feeling. She'd attached a dozen or so photos, most of them taken at a waterfall and a few in front of what appeared to be a forest of bamboo. She was glad to see they were having fun.

"I don't mind resting for a bit, but then I'd better get back and be there before the girls come looking for me," she said. "I haven't answered Laura's text message yet and I sure don't need another lecture for not being there when they get to the cabin."

Betty chuckled. "It must be nice to have daughters who care about you and are always looking out for you."

"Well, yes, I suppose so. Though sometimes I wish they'd remember who the parent is."

"I can see how that would be tricky, too," Betty said, nodding at her as she braked for a trail of tourists crossing the road. "With your husband gone, I'm sure they're having a difficult time knowing how to navigate what to do in his place."

"That's just it. They don't need to do anything. Not right now, anyway. I'm perfectly capable of taking care of myself. I think they want to get me out of my home and there's no reason for that yet. I just need to find my footing—not relocate it."

"Maybe a long, serious talk is warranted," Betty said, her eyes on the road again. "Could you set down some new ground rules and possibly satisfy some of their worries?"

"I don't know," Caroline said. "I'm just not in a headspace right now to take them on if they're going to gang up on me. I need them to see that I want their emotional support, but I don't want them taking over my life."

"Is there some reason they feel the need to step in? Maybe they've seen you struggling since your husband's passing?"

Caroline hesitated. Could it be possible that her depression and reluctance to do anything with herself, or for herself, had acted as a red flag that put in motion the talks the girls were having? Could it be her fault that they were trying to bulldoze in and change her life?

"I'm really not sure," she replied. But Betty had given her something to think about.

"I just remembered, Gracie told me to invite you to our family picnic tonight," Betty said. "I know you may have something else you want to do, but if not, the girls are welcome too. You could all see what a real Hawaiian picnic is all about."

"That's so kind of you both. I'll ask the girls."

"Forewarning," Betty said, glancing at her and winking, "if your girls are vegetarian, they'll need to be prepared for the shock of seeing a kalua pig being cooked in the underground oven. But there will be plenty of non-meat dishes, too. We usually have music, and dancing always breaks out before it's over with, too."

"It sounds like fun. What do we wear?"

"Whatever you'd like," Betty said. "It'll be on the beach and it's very casual. Tell them to bring their swimsuits if they want to get in the water."

"I'll do that. I know Rachel will probably want to swim. Not sure about the other two."

Suddenly, Betty asked Caroline a loaded question.

"So, tell me about your home life now. What keeps you busy?"

Caroline hesitated. Nothing really kept her busy now that James was gone. She'd never realized how much their schedules wrapped around what he wanted to do or taking care of him in some way. Doing his laundry. Planning and executing their meals. Collaborating on his constant special projects or at least trying to dissuade him from the ones that seemed impossible to pull off.

Now she spent some of her day walking around the house aimlessly, not knowing what to do to pass the time. Even thinking about it made her feel pathetic.

"I have two cats," she finally said. "They're fairly persistent about their needs, I guess you could say."

"Oh, that's right. I forgot you're with the cat crowd on the boat," Betty said. "What's their names?"

"Felix and Fauci."

Betty laughed. "So, you're a cat person, then. I have a dog. A tiny little Yorkie that thinks he's a massive rottweiler and who is probably terrorizing his pet sitter as we speak. His name is Theo."

Caroline laughed. She'd seen little dogs like that. "Well, I wasn't a cat person at all and not sure if I still am, but since I've been away from them for a few days I guess you could say I might be leaning that way. I miss them terribly. Luckily for them, though, they love my neighbor and she's their sitter for this trip."

"If you're missing your felines, I have just the thing to do but we need to start early. Tomorrow if you want to come out with me, we can take the ferry to the small island of Lana'i

and visit the cat sanctuary," Betty said.

"A cat sanctuary?"

She nodded. "Absolutely. They have more than six hundred cats they care for, and they have built the perfect reserve for them."

"I haven't heard of Lana'i," Caroline said. "Did it have a cat problem?"

"Somewhat. The founder, Kathy Carroll, wanted to find a way to protect the island's cats as well as the endangered birds. First, they sheltered the cats in an old horse corral up in Koele, but eventually they moved to where they are now, more than three acres of cat paradise."

"Is the whole island just about cats?"

Betty glanced over at her and laughed. "Lord, no. It's an island that caters to tourists. There's a fancy golf course and a Four Seasons Resort. It's also a great place to go diving because its north side has Shipwreck Beach, where there's an offshore wreck of a WWII tanker and Mike Carroll has a lovely gallery there and you can buy his famous prints. We can have lunch at the Blue Ginger. I haven't been there in ages and the owners probably think I've kicked the bucket by now. Won't they be surprised?"

Caroline chuckled. "How long does it take to get there?"

"About forty-five minutes or so. It's a nice ride, though. We might even see some whales breaching. I'll book the tickets tonight if you're interested?"

"I'd love that," Caroline said. The girls wouldn't be happy with her decision, but they'd have to live with it. It would just give them one more day to do whatever they wanted without minding her limitations.

"I'm so glad that—" before Betty could finish her sentence, Caroline saw a blur of red in front of the car.

Betty hit the brakes, sending them into a screeching slide for what felt like an eternity before the loud sound of the two vehicles making impact against each other drowned everything else out.

Seven

Caroline had never put together a bucket list but if she had, it would be a reverse list of all the things you never want to do, and riding in an ambulance through afternoon traffic on Maui would be at the top. She had thought they'd end up in another wreck before they'd even made it to the hospital.

Her first and hopefully last ride in an ambulance was a doozy. Now, after seven hours of x-rays, exams, and then waiting in the lobby for Gracie's nephew to come pick them up, they'd arrived back at the house. Betty, unfortunately, was released with a broken foot and cracked kneecap, but Caroline was lucky with only bruises and a sore neck.

"Thank you for coming to get us, Jorge," Betty said to her nephew as he assisted with getting her out of the car.

Gracie met them in the driveway and was supervising over his shoulder.

"Of course. I came as soon as Gracie called," he said. "That's what family does."

"I'll get you settled in my room on the first floor," Gracie said to Betty.

"No, I'll be okay in the parlor for now," Betty said, struggling to get the crutches under her arm and her feet steady beneath her. "I'll wait until these pain meds kick in before I try to lay down."

Caroline stood watching and feeling helpless. Her soreness was already setting in, especially where the seatbelt had caught her across her chest and neck, but Betty had gotten the brunt of the injuries.

"It's a miracle you two weren't hurt worse or even killed," Jorge said. "I saw the wreckage on my way home and both of the vehicles are totaled."

"He pulled right out in front of us," Caroline said. "There wasn't time to even stop."

"I owe you a car," Betty said, looking up at her sister.

Caroline felt the heat rise up her neck and into her cheeks. The accident wouldn't have happened at all if Betty hadn't borrowed the car to show her around the island.

"Psst. I don't care about that old thing," Gracie said. "I'll find something else to go galivanting around in. I'm just glad you're both okay. I mean, other than your broken foot and chipped kneecap."

"Lean on me and I'll lift you up each step," Jorge said as they approached the porch.

The doctor claimed surgery wasn't needed, but he'd put Betty into a stabilizing big black boot that encased her foot and leg up to the knee instead of casting it. He said casting would make it more likely for infection to set in and that the boot would make it easier to bathe and move around. He gave strict instructions for Betty to stay off the foot as much as possible for the first week, then to come back and let him x-ray it again before she could travel.

Before they could all get into the house, a car pulled up and parked beside Jorge's car.

Caroline turned to see the doors fly open and her girls climbing out, the driver out last and following them.

"We'll see you inside," Betty said, giving Caroline a look of support before disappearing into the house with Jorge and Gracie.

Caroline wasn't so sure she wanted to be alone with her daughters just yet. The call she'd made to them from the hospital had gone to voicemail, and she'd followed up with a text message that gave them the outline of what happened and the address of Gracie's house. Hopefully they'd be calmed down by now.

Rachel was first up the steps onto the porch and just about knocked her off the ground in a bear hug. "Mama! We were so worried!"

"What in God's name were you doing out riding around?" Peggy said. "You told us you were staying on board. Otherwise, we wouldn't have left you."

Laura moved in to push Rachel aside and hugged Caroline. "You've given us quite a scare, Mom, but thank God you're okay. How is Betty? Where were you going? Why didn't you tell us you weren't staying on the boat?"

Caroline pushed her way out of the pack and gestured at the porch swing and chairs.

"Sit, please. I'll tell you everything if you'll calm down."

"Let me tell the driver something," Peggy said. "Should he wait?"

"No," Caroline said. "I'm not leaving Betty yet. She said we could all hang out here for the evening. Gracie said that family members will be bringing by a ton of food once word gets out about Betty being here and the accident. You girls can go back to the ship now if you'd like, or you can stay, and we can taxi back together later."

"I'm not leaving you again," Peggy said. "Who knows what you'll get into."

"Same," Laura and Rachel agreed. They weren't budging.

"Don't tell anything until I get back," Peggy said, then went and talked to the driver. She got out her purse and handed over some bills, then returned to the porch as he backed out of the driveway.

She settled into a chair, then crossed her arms over her chest. "Now, talk. I can't even imagine what's gotten into you, Mom. I mean, wow—who do you and Betty think you are? Thelma and Louise of the high blue seas? What's next? Are you to planning to jump overboard in a last big hurrah?"

Caroline could tell by her tone that Peggy wasn't trying to be funny, but she laughed anyway, to try to break the ice. "Well, not quite. I ran into Betty when I was watching guests disembark this morning and she talked me into coming into town with her instead of staying on board. It's as simple as that. We did some sightseeing and were just about back here when a truck ran out in front of us, and we crashed. The car was totaled. We didn't die. End of story."

"That's not the end of the story," Laura said. "You could've been killed. And if you were hurt more seriously and couldn't text or call us, no one would've known who to contact. We would've been out of our minds if we'd gone back to the ship, and you were missing."

"Well, none of that happened so let's just stop thinking of what could have been," Caroline said. "I'm sorry that I gave you all a scare, but right now I'm worried about my friend. She's the one with broken bones and probably won't be able to finish the cruise. Not to mention she's very upset about totaling her sister's only vehicle. For just a minute can we think of someone other than ourselves?"

Her speech did the trick and the girls stopped badgering her. Caroline did feel guilty—if the tables were turned, and they'd gone off the ship and gotten into an accident when she thought they were safely on board, she could see herself getting upset, too. However, what was done was done and anyway, if they'd have acted as though they wanted her with them to go around Maui, none of this would have happened.

Not that she'd rub that in their faces.

"I'm sorry, girls," Caroline said, sighing loudly. "I don't mean to be so short with you, but I feel terrible about Betty's injuries and the car. It feels like I'm responsible."

"Mom—" the three of them rushed to console her and tell her it wasn't her fault, but Caroline still felt guilty. The house that Gracie lived in was cozy and modest, and the car was at least ten years old, but it was obvious that it was well taken care of.

Gracie didn't appear to be a woman of means who could just rush out and buy a replacement vehicle.

Caroline was saved from more of their empty reassurances by a trio of ladies coming up the walkway, their arms full. "Aloha," they called out, then climbed the porch and went on into the house, as though they lived there.

A whiff of all sorts of delicious aromas floated up and lingered behind them.

"So..." Rachel said, trailing off as though looking for a new conversation point and avoiding the possibility that she might get the cabin to herself for the remaining cruise. "Did we tell you about the insanely good lunch we had yesterday? They called it Huli Huli chicken, and it was cooked right there on the side of the road."

Caroline smiled at her youngest daughter, then listened as they raved about how the plates were only twenty dollars each but could've fed several, and then the picnic table overlooking a scene that could've been out of a postcard, where they sat and ate together.

It sounded like they'd made some good memories on the Road to Hana and that made her happy, even if she wasn't a part of them. They talked about a local who dived off a tall rock at Black Sand Beach, and them walking through a magical bamboo garden that sounded peaceful.

"And we stood under a waterfall," Laura said.

"It took us forever to convince Peggy to get her feet

wet, then she slipped and fell in. She lost a shoe and I had to find it," Rachel said, laughing at the memory.

Peggy chuckled. "I wasn't leaving without that water shoe. Those were a splurge for the trip."

"Coincidentally enough, they didn't hold up any better than my ten-dollar drugstore shoes," Laura said.

"You don't know that," Peggy said. "That brand is proven to keep your feet drier for longer. If they stay on, I mean."

"I told you to take them off first," Rachel said. "Part of the experience is feeling the water between your toes. How can you do that when they are encased in shoes, whether they cost a hundred dollars or ten?"

"I'm glad you girls enjoyed yourselves," Caroline said, diverting the direction of the conversation. "See how wonderful it can be when you put your differences aside and just live in the moment?"

"That's what I told them," Rachel said. "They started up first thing, fussing over where to stop for lunch, but the driver settled it when he said he knew the best place. And he was right. I'd even go back for that chicken again."

"I wouldn't," Peggy said. "You'll never get me on the Road to Hana again. Those blind curves had me clenching every body part I could find."

The girls laughed.

"While we're all here, can we talk about what to plan for the Hilo port call tomorrow?" Peggy asked. "It will be easier if I can go ahead and book any excursions sometime today."

"I'd like to go downtown and browse around,"

Rachel said. "Supposedly, it's less touristy than Maui's Front Street and many of the old storefronts are still there and designated on the National Historic registry."

"That sounds interesting, if Mom's not too sore to walk around," Peggy said. "I was talking to a man yesterday who said we can't miss the waterfalls in the Akaka Falls State Park."

On the opposite side of the street, two fellows got out of a car. They popped the trunk and one pulled out a walker while the other lifted out a large ice cooler. They approached, nodded a greeting, then followed the trio of ladies into the house.

"Something's going on," Rachel said, watching them go by.

"There was supposed to be a family get-together on the beach. I'm guessing because of the accident, it's being moved to here," Caroline said.

Gracie peeked out the door. "You guessed right, Caroline. They're setting up out back if you girls want to come help out."

Then she shut the door.

"We aren't staying, are we?" Peggy asked. "I told Richard to come back for us in an hour. I thought we'd be going back to the ship for dinner. Mom, when the soreness from the accident sets in, you're going to be in trouble. We need to get you settled in."

"You girls go on without me," Caroline said. She refrained from telling them that the soreness was already setting in. "I'm staying. I want to make sure that Betty is set up and comfortable before I skulk away with my tail between my legs."

"Mom—I'm sure no one blames you," Laura said. "You said it was the other guy's fault."

The screen door behind them opened and Gracie stepped out.

"Caroline, it absolutely was not your fault and don't you worry a bit about that old car. I wanted to get something different anyway. I'm relieved that you are all okay for the most part, and the whole thing has just spurred me on to look for something that fits me better."

"You are too kind," Caroline said, still feeling embarrassed, especially that Gracie had caught them talking about the loss of her car.

"Please, I'd like for all of you to stay and enjoy an afternoon and evening of fellowship. You'll learn more about Hawaii by doing that than any excursion you can book. Hang out and meet my friends. Listen to my family talk story, and I promise you won't regret it. I think Betty would like that, too." Gracie said.

Caroline could see that it was important to Gracie, and she made an executive decision.

"Thank you, we accept your invitation. The girls and I would be honored to stay and meet your friends and family."

She gave the girls a look that dared them to argue, and thankfully they nodded in agreement. Even Peggy, who Caroline could tell was just biting at the bit to say something different.

Gracie smiled broadly. "Great. Come on around back when you're ready. There're a few people out there setting up now and I'd better hurry up and make sure it's going alright."

She left them.

Despite feeling stiff and sore, Caroline was genuinely enjoying the event and sat next to Betty and Gracie in a circle of friends. At least forty or more people had showed up, most all of them carrying covered dishes and a chair to sit in. The pig was cooked elsewhere and then brought over, sliced and laid out on colorful platters garnished with pineapple. A dessert table was also set up and after eating too many helpings of the main dishes, including the traditional macaroni salad, Caroline had already indulged in the sweets. Her favorite was the malasada, a donut-like concoction that was filled with banana custard. She could've gone for at least half a dozen of them but refrained and settled for a tiny sliver of chocolate Haupia pie, mostly because Gracie had made it and insisted that Caroline had to try it before leaving Maui.

Betty sat next to her and leaned closer. "Caroline, I have something really important to talk to you about before you leave tonight."

"Oh? What's it about?" Caroline felt a nervous flutter in her stomach. Was Betty going to talk to her about the accident? Ask for help in replacing her sister's car?

"I don't want to get into it here where everyone can listen in," Betty said. "We'll find us a quiet corner later and talk. Just enjoy yourself for now. Have you had enough to eat?"

"Oh goodness, yes," Caroline said. "Too much, actually."

The girls had raved over the liliko'i bars, the island's version of lemon bars, and Caroline was thinking about having another round at them.

Everything was really nice. Food *and* company. Even Peggy, the hardest to please of the bunch, seemed to be really enjoying the evening and as far as Caroline could see, was even staying off her phone.

The event was better than sightseeing. Caroline felt like she was experiencing the real Maui. Not just the tourist traps and the paradise of manicured resort grounds and such. Here, children ran about, playing and laughing, some barefoot and fancy free. A trio of teenagers huddled together on the porch, their heads dipped over their cell phones, a burst of laughter ringing out occasionally, when one shared something they thought funny.

Across the way, an older man played a guitar and sang softly, a melodic Hawaiian tune that Caroline couldn't quite make out over the conversation they were having about the qualms of getting older. A younger man sat next to him, a ukulele offering a traditional and interesting accompaniment to the strumming of the guitar.

Betty shifted in her seat, moving her booted leg a bit higher on the footstool someone had placed there for her as she spoke again, reminding Caroline that they were talking about the trials of old age.

Betty gestured with her hands as she talked. "For me, it's simple. My seventy-year-old self enjoys most of the same things that my fifty-year-old self did, and I try my best to keep doing them. I learned a long time ago that it's all about keeping moving so things don't rust and go to pot. I hate the gym so instead, I walk my dog twice a day—once in the morning and once in the evening, and I use small weights a few times a week to keep my arm and core muscle tone going. In the mornings I listen to music to keep up my mood. I let myself enjoy the long naps I've earned during my lifetime, and I read more than I've ever read in my life because I never get tired of learning."

A woman named Helen nodded emphatically. "I do that, too. My book club is the highlight of my month. But the hardest part of getting old for me is losing people in my life. I know we are all going to die but when you're young, you don't realize how many funerals you'll attend one day for people who are in the same generation as you. It happens at too frequent a pace to keep up these days."

Betty gave Caroline a sympathetic smile. "I'm sorry, friend. I know that's what you are dealing with right now. The loss of a husband is so much harder than the loss of anyone in your life, other than a child."

"I know how you feel," Gracie said. "They say that grief is the price we pay for love, and I believe that's truer than most people ever have to find out."

"I just miss him so much," Caroline said. "And I've always believed in an afterlife, but now that he's gone, I find myself worrying about where he is now and if he's okay. It hurts me to think of him in the cold ground."

"You could always ask Yoshie about him," Helen said. "There she is, right there." She pointed in the direction of a slim, dark-haired woman who heard her name and turned to look.

"Someone call out to me?" she asked.

Helen gestured to her, and the woman slowly made her way over.

"Yoshie, this is Caroline and her daughters, from the mainland," Helen said. "Betty met them on the cruise ship that's in port tonight."

Caroline was glad Helen didn't go into the details of the accident again. It had already been scrutinized and investigated by at least a dozen people within earshot at the party so far. Everyone had an opinion about the danger of that intersection, and a few people even knew the guy who hit them, and reported he was doing fine with no injuries but was lamenting over the damage to his old truck.

It seemed Maui was a smaller town that she'd realized.

"Hello to you all," Yoshie said. "How do you like Maui?"

"It's beautiful, what I've seen of it," Caroline said. The girls nodded, too.

"Caroline just lost her husband recently," Gracie said, nodding knowingly at Yoshie.

The girls happened to sidle up at that moment and Rachel took an empty chair in the circle while Laura and Peggy hovered behind the circle.

"Oh, well I don't really do impromptu readings anymore," Yoshie said. She looked genuinely sorry.

"Helen didn't know you don't do unscheduled readings. I'm sorry," Gracie said. "Please, just enjoy the party."

"I apologize," Helen said. "I just thought—well,

you're here. And she's here and struggling. You know. A reading wouldn't hurt."

Caroline wanted to melt into her chair. Helen was pushy.

"Readings?" Rachel asked. "What do you mean?"

"Yoshi is a medium and a psychic," Helen said. "She's very well known on the islands."

Peggy let out a harsh chuckle. "We don't believe in that stuff. It's against our religion."

"Speak for yourself," Rachel said. "I believe. And that doesn't make me a heathen. It makes me open to possibilities that as the average human, we can't understand."

Peggy was taken aback, and Yoshie looked self-conscious.

"I'm so sorry," Caroline apologized. "Please excuse my daughter. She doesn't mean to be rude, she's just outspoken."

She shrugged. "No need to apologize. Skeptics are a big part of my life and one of the reasons I don't do impromptu readings. These days I don't feel the need to prove myself to anyone."

"Oh, she's real," Helen said. "She studied at the world's largest spiritualist organization."

"Pray tell, where is that?" Peggy asked, her tone laced with sarcasm.

"Great Britain," Yoshie replied.

"Ooh, I love this kind of stuff," Rachel said. "But what is the difference between a psychic and a medium?"

"I know that one," Laura said. "Mediums talk to ghosts."

Yoshie chuckled. "You're not wrong. Psychics connect with energy fields from the aura of the live person they are reading. Everyone can be a psychic if they learn how to tap into their abilities. Mediums are psychic, too, but they can also connect with spirits from the other side."

Caroline felt a sense of the bottom falling out from under her feet. She had never in her life thought about psychics or mediums. Not until James died.

Then she had thought about them quite a bit, though she'd never admit it.

But that still didn't make her a believer.

"Can you talk to our dad?" Rachel asked.

Everyone around them went silent and Yoshi hesitated, then turned her attention to Caroline. "Are you open to a message from him? I mean, I don't usually do this, but I am getting a strong sense that he's trying to connect."

Caroline froze. Was she open to something like this? She didn't really believe, so it couldn't hurt, right?

"Mom, don't do this," Peggy said.

"Stop telling her what to do," Rachel said, her expression angry.

Laura put her hand on Caroline's wrist. "Do what you want, Mom. It might bring you some peace."

Yoshie waited patiently.

Caroline smiled and shrugged as though she were accepting an invitation to play a game. "Sure. Why not?"

"First, he says thank you for taking the trip," Yoshie said.

Caroline nodded. Just about everyone at the get

together knew they were from a cruise, so that wasn't anything earth-shattering.

"Because you didn't want to," Yoshie continued. And he says he's with you. He wants you to look for the dimes. Do you understand that?"

Despite the muggy heat, Caroline felt a chill run up her arms, all the way to her head.

"I—well, I—" she mumbled.

She hadn't told anyone about the dimes. Not the first one she'd seen on the ship and not the one she'd seen in the water that day. But how common was it to find a dime? Or two?

"You may not know what the connection is right now but hold on to this message and you might figure it out later," Yoshie said, her voice soft and comforting. "He wants you to stop wishing you could turn back time and start rebuilding your life in a way that's for yourself."

Caroline was speechless, but she kept her cards close to the vest and didn't let on that anything substantial was said.

"Do you have anything else?" Rachel asked. "Is he still here?"

Beside her, Peggy rolled her eyes, then walked away.

Laura waited silently.

"He's here. Just one more thing. A word he keeps saying to me while he laughs," Yoshi said. "It's silly. Some kind of joke, I think. I'm not really sure what to make of it, or if it's even anything important."

"What is it?" Rachel said.

Yoshie looked embarrassed. "Meow."

Eight

The morning Maui sun was brutal, even in the shady parts of the ship and guests were up early to get ready to tackle their last day on the island. Caroline was nervous and didn't feel like eating breakfast, but she picked at a few of the items she'd piled on her plate. Everyone was absolutely right and the next day after an accident was the worst. In addition to her frayed nerves, she hurt from her nose to her toes and could only imagine how much pain Betty was in with her broken foot and chipped kneecap.

When they'd returned to the ship the night before, she had shut down the conversation about Yoshie and her message, especially since her own thoughts had been on the private conversation she and Betty had had before they'd left Gracie's cookout.

Betty had made a request of Caroline that had at first seemed impossible.

Now she wasn't so sure.

She told Betty she'd think on it.

This morning the girls were all about dissecting the message from the medium. Except for Rachel, who looked at it as a gift and not something to try to prove wrong.

"Betty probably told her that you're on the cat cruise," Peggy said. "That's why she said meow."

"Probably," Caroline said, though she didn't believe it. Even if Betty had told the medium that detail, no one else knew about the dimes. Not before Yoshie said it and not even now.

Caroline wasn't ready to share that. She didn't even know what to think about it herself and today, she had something else more pressing to tell her daughters.

"That's easy enough to verify," Peggy said. "Did you get Betty's phone number? We'll call her."

"Would you two stop?" Rachel said, sighing loudly. "Just leave it alone and let her message be a comfort to Mom."

Caroline wasn't sure if it was a comfort or not—first she had to decide if she believed it.

"I just don't like how these frauds get away playing on people's emotions," Peggy said.

"I did get Betty's number, but I'm not going to bother her about that. I'll see her later today but that's the last thing I want to talk about," Caroline said.

The girls perked up.

"You're seeing her later? Mom, we don't have time to stop by there before the snorkeling excursion," Peggy said. "We can't be late."

"Are you going with us on the boat?" Laura asked. "According to reviews, it's the best charter to book. They call it *The Trilogy* and it's big enough that I don't think any of us will get seasick."

"That's what I need to talk to you girls about. Well, that and a few other things."

They all looked at her expectedly.

"I won't be going with you today, and as a matter of fact, I won't be finishing out the cruise at all," Caroline said, then reminded herself to breathe.

A server was approaching the table with a tray to remove some of the dishes, but he backed away when he saw their serious expressions.

"What do you mean?" Laura asked.

"Betty doesn't want to try to continue the cruise. She wants to fly home and has asked me to escort her, help her get settled, then fly on to Colorado Springs from there. I feel like it's the least I can do, considering if not for taking me out and about, this accident wouldn't have happened."

Caroline could see a range of emotions flutter across the faces of the girls.

"You can't just leave the ship at port and not return," Peggy said. "They'd think they have a missing passenger. Can you imagine the chaos?"

"I know that," Caroline said. "Gracie already checked into it, and I have to go talk to the Guest Flight Operations office this morning and complete paperwork to get special clearance. They've already done it for Betty. They'll probably charge what's called a PVSA fine, but I'm okay with that. We plan to stay on Maui for at least another week to let Betty get used to getting around with the boot, then we'll fly to the mainland."

"I don't like this one bit," Peggy said.

"I have to agree," Laura chimed in. "Anything could happen, and we'd never know."

Rachel looked shocked.

"I'm not asking your permission," Caroline said softly. "And that's the other thing I want to talk to you about. Just because your father is gone doesn't mean that I need you girls stepping in to try to run my life."

Rachel put her hand on Caroline's wrist. "Mom, we are just worried about you."

"I know you are. And that's probably a lot my fault, too. I've been a mess and I admit that. I've been walking around like a zombie. But I'm ready to put on my big girl pants and get on with life now."

"I don't think you're in any condition to take off on your own," Rachel said. "At least let one of us go, too. I can fly back with you both."

"Thank you, but we'll be fine. I'll be fine," Caroline said. "Matter of fact, I'm better than fine. Spending time with Betty has opened my eyes and made me realize that yes, burying your father has been a challenge and yes, I'm old and can't do a lot of the things I used to do. But I'm not dead—and I have to stop acting like it. I don't plan on doing anything crazy like get a dozen cats or find an Internet boyfriend. Nothing like that. However, I'm going to make my own decisions and if I want to stay in my big, empty home and stare at the walls, I'll do that, too. I'm not selling it."

Peggy sat back in her chair and crossed her arms over her chest.

"Yep, Peggy, I heard some of what the three of you

were planning to talk to me about. I appreciate that you understand the real estate market and if and when I ever decide to sell the house that your father and I worked so hard to make into a home, you'll be the first one I call."

"No one planned to force you to do anything, Mom," Peggy said. "But there are places you can live where you can have things to do, people to talk to."

"Without worrying about keeping up the yard or the house," Laura added.

"And I might consider one of those places one day," Caroline said. "But not today. And not tomorrow. Maybe never, or at least not until I'm good and ready."

"You might miss out on a seller's market," Peggy said. "Could be the best price you'll ever get for the house is right now."

"I don't care about that," Caroline said. "As you girls know, we aren't wealthy, but we also aren't in a pickle. I'll be fine whether I sell the house or keep it."

"Sounds to me like you have your mind made up," Rachel said.

Caroline nodded. "I sure do. It's made up about accompanying Betty to California and made up to take things slow until I feel ready to tackle life again. On my terms and not anyone else's. However, Betty gave me the name of her financial manager and I'm going to call and make an appointment for a consultation, just to set my mind at ease about where I stand with your dad gone."

"I think that's a fabulous idea," Rachel said. "They'll be able to tell you if you need to buckle down and stay on a budget, or if you've got enough to do more cruises."

"I don't think I'll be taking any more cruises," Caroline said. "This was really going to be for your dad. I'd feel better keeping my feet on the ground. But that doesn't mean I won't want to do any traveling at all. And you never know, I might decide I like California enough to live there. Betty sure thinks it's the bee's knees."

That got their attention. They looked panicked for a moment. Or at least Laura and Peggy did. Rachel got an interested gleam in her eyes.

"That would be really cool," she said. "No more winters. I might join you, too."

"Don't encourage her," Peggy said to Rachel. "Mom, you just told us you don't want to sell your house and now you're talking about moving to California?"

"I didn't *talk about* moving. I'm just saying, all my options are open and I'm not crossing anything off the list of possibilities. It's not like I'm that involved in your lives where I must stay in Colorado. You are all busy with your own families. When is the last time you invited me to watch one of the kids play in their after school stuff? Or asked me to dinner on a regular night and not just for a holiday?"

"We didn't think you'd want to come," Laura said. "It's all so exhausting, I don't even want to do it myself."

"I may not always say yes, but I'd like to be asked," Caroline said. "Otherwise, what's the point of me living in the same town? I can see the photos on the Internet from anywhere, just fine."

"But we like having you close," Laura said. "Just in case."

Peggy and Rachel nodded.

"Glad to see you all agreeing on something," Caroline said. She took a long sip from her coffee mug. "That brings me to the last thing I want to talk to you about today. If I've learned anything in the last several months, it's that we shouldn't waste time. The three of you are grown women, yet you spend more time bickering with or about each other than you do enjoying the time you have together."

She was pleased to see that they looked sufficiently guilty.

"Laura, you see Peggy as someone who has many of the things you want now, but you don't realize that she's already been in your shoes, and you'll get there eventually. And Peggy, you forget how much of a struggle it was just to get by when your kids were younger. You didn't have time for top-notch parenting, meals, and making your house envy-worthy. Cut your sister some slack, or better yet, step in to help her," Caroline said.

Peggy let out a long, slow breath. "You're right. Laura, I'm an idiot. And to tell you the truth, I'm kind of jealous that your kids are young and still want to do things like crawl into bed with you at night or have you at every sideline event. I wish I still had those days. Mine are rarely home anymore."

"What?" Laura said. "Are you crazy? You and Scott get to have date night once a week, and you can shut the door and take a hot bath without little people parking next to the tub and asking you a billion questions like 'Why is the sky blue?' and 'Why don't crabs have eyebrows?' You can run around the house naked if you want and I can't even eat a meal without someone picking the best parts off my plate."

"To be honest, I miss those inane questions," Peggy said, sighing loudly.

Rachel laughed sardonically. "Well, both of you don't realize how lucky you are. How would you like to come home to an empty apartment every night? You think being footloose and fancy free is so awesome, but let me tell you, it can get lonely fast. Neither of you ever ask me to the kids' stuff, either. Here's a tip; I like school plays and soccer games. Especially when I can cheer on my nieces and nephews."

"We always think you're out with friends, doing fun, single stuff," Laura insisted. "It would be nice to have someone to sit with when Scott's out of town."

"You should've said something," Peggy said.

Caroline could see something in her girls' eyes that she wasn't used to seeing.

They were sympathizing with each other.

Showing compassion instead of competition.

"What we need to realize is that there's nothing to be envious of. None of us have a perfect life," Caroline said. "But what we do still have is each other. That won't always be true, and I just want you girls to stop wasting time on the silly stuff. I want you to be more than sisters. You should be friends. No one in this world will ever know you like a sister does and you have all taken it for granted."

They were quiet. Another miracle that didn't happen often.

"We've taken you for granted, too, Mom," Peggy finally said. "I'm sorry I didn't see that you felt left out of our lives. I'm sorry that I've been so busy to notice anything other than what's right under my nose, and we also shouldn't have been talking about your finances behind your back."

"I'm sorry too, Mom," Laura said. "I'll start asking you to everything. The kids would love to have you there. I promise I'll stop trying to boss you around, too."

"I'll hold you all to that," Caroline said. "Until I give some indication that I'm not of sound body and mind, I'm still your mother and you'll still show me the respect I'm due. If and when I ever falter, then we'll talk about how the three of you can help me navigate the last years of my life. But don't count me out yet, girls. I still know a thing or three."

They all nodded in agreement and Caroline could've sworn they looked relieved. Perhaps they weren't so eager after all to run her affairs.

Peggy turned to Laura, "And I think you're doing a wonderful job with your kids. I really do. It's just that I like being the older sister and I can't help but give advice. I'll work on that and I'm sorry I can be such an ass sometimes. The truth is, I know I've been hard to deal with and I don't even like myself. I've been struggling with my marriage and didn't want you guys to know. We haven't had too many date nights and haven't wanted them, either. So I've been a jerk to cover it up."

Caroline could see tears welling up in her eldest daughter's eyes and it pained her to think that Peggy had been suffering silently with marital issues. She'd always tried to keep things to herself, though. But what was the good in having sisters if you couldn't confide and commiserate with them?

"Agreed and apology accepted," Laura said. "Seriously, though. I'm sorry things have been rough. I'm here if you want to talk through it. You never know, I can possibly help, and I would've already tried if you hadn't always tried to pretend like everything is so perfect. Oh, and you're welcome to have the girls over any time you want, and I promise they'll cuddle and binge watch something silly on the television with you. Just be careful what you wish for, or they'll be there every weekend. They think you are so much cooler than I am."

"But not as cool as their Aunt Rachel," Rachel said, winking at them. "I don't wear mom jeans and I don't care what time they go to bed."

They all laughed.

"Remember that time we didn't speak for three months because I thought we shouldn't have to pay exactly half the dinner out when our kids were splitting a plate, and yours weren't and they also ordered appetizers?" Laura asked Peggy. "Months we wasted!"

"Well, to be fair, you two were drinking and we thought that made it balance out. I was so confused that you were mad," Peggy said. "We should've talked it out instead of just being resentful at each other. We've been idiots. Why couldn't we see it?"

"Family members always take each other for granted," Caroline said. She wasn't even going to mention the macaroni and cheese debate. It was best not to raise some spats from the dead. "Until it's too late to do anything about it. But we can start now to undo the patterns and try to live differently. To love differently," Caroline said.

They all thought about that for a minute.

"Mom, I think Dad would be really proud of you right now," Rachel said. "Acting independent and forcing us to like each other again."

They laughed.

"He'd probably wonder what the heck has gotten into you," Laura said. "You always let him take the lead."

"Not always," Peggy said. "I do seem to recall you finally convincing him to buy a GPS system for your old car."

Caroline smiled. "It took a while. He always said that they were designed by college kids with no sense of direction. He said they couldn't possibly know all the good shortcuts he had stored in his memory from decades of living around the state."

"Remember his old atlas?" Peggy said. "It's been put back together with duct tape so many times it looks like it's been ripped apart by wolves."

"Dad hated asking directions," Rachel said.

"All men do," both Laura and Peggy said at the same time.

"Jinx." They both followed up with, then burst into laughter.

Caroline smiled. "He would love to see this, you know. You all laughing together. It pained him so much to hear about you girls scrapping at each other all the time. He always said you'd grow out of it, though. We've always wanted you girls to turn *to* each other, not against each other."

"That needs to be the new goal," Rachel said. "I'm going to declare Dad as right and say we've outgrown all that. Manifest it, put it into the universe and all that."

"They don't make 'em like Dad anymore," Laura said.

"They sure don't. Remember how he always had the exact change to pay for stuff, no matter what it was?" Peggy said. "He jangled when he walked."

They all nodded.

"That's because he was so crazy about those coins. He always had a pocketful," Caroline said. "Every night he'd empty them on the table and go through them so carefully, looking for one that would make us rich."

"I think Dad is here with us right now," Rachel said. "Just like Yoshie said."

Caroline thought about the dimes, and she reached under the table to pat her pocket. She'd slipped them in there before leaving the cabin. She was going to need a lot more pants with pockets because she didn't want to be without the coins again.

"I think you're right," she agreed. "He's watching over us. And he's probably reminding me that I need to get a move on. I have a lot to accomplish today while you girls are out venturing around. I can't believe I'm going to be on Maui for a whole week."

Betty had acted like she was the one who needed Caroline, but something told Caroline that the request was more than that.

Rachel suddenly bounced in her seat, smiling ear to ear.

"Guess what I just thought of?" she asked. When no one offered up anything, her smile turned ornery. "I'm going to get the bed—and the cabin—all to myself."

Epilogue

San Francisco was gorgeous and exciting, and a wonderful place to relax, but it wasn't Colorado Springs and Caroline was feeling more homesick each day. Only one more sleep and she'd be on her way.

She looked around the apartment at all her new friends that felt like old friends, and she knew she'd miss them. A week on Maui and then the impromptu three weeks with Betty in California had opened her eyes to a whole new way of living.

"Thank you all so much for today. I really didn't expect a send-off party," Caroline said, lifting her margarita glass in a toast of thanks.

Betty took it as a request for a refill and she lifted the pitcher.

"No, that's enough. It's getting late and I have to get up early for my flight. I sure don't want to carry a hangover home. The girls will already be picking over me to see if they think I've turned into some crazy West Coast chick."

They laughed at her, and Caroline remembered the first night they'd introduced her to margaritas and how she'd barely made it to the guest room without staggering. She'd learned to pace herself over the last few weeks, and to pretend like she was keeping up instead of really doing so. Betty and her friends thought she was a lightweight and they were right. Caroline wasn't ever going to be a drinker, and that was okay. She'd be fine with a strong cup of chai tea and a fat novel, though it had been a fun time getting to know another way of life and witnessing others her age and older enjoying themselves.

"And you promise you'll come back for the Polk Street Blues Festival," Vera said. "Or I'll come get you myself. I always wanted to sled down a mountain of snow."

Vera had never lived anywhere with cold weather and Caroline would love to talk her into a visit to Colorado.

"I'll be here with bells on," Caroline said. That was something else she'd discovered in California. She loved listening to blues music. Though James loved to dance, he'd never been one to follow music, even when they were younger, and Caroline was surprised at how much she enjoyed it now. Especially the live events. The music and the beat flowed through her and made her feel alive again. Music was certainly a gift she planned on taking back to Colorado.

One by one, the ladies embraced Caroline and said their goodbyes before slipping out the door, until it was just her and Betty left.

"Now I can put my feet up and we can have one more long talk before I excuse myself to go wrap my leg and take a shower," Betty said, then made her way somewhat spryly across the living room to her recliner.

Caroline took the sofa across from her. She was tired, emotionally and physically, and glad that most of her packing was already done and she could wash up and get in bed soon.

Just as suspected, Betty hadn't really needed a caregiver when she'd asked Caroline to accompany her back to California. She hadn't wanted to finish the cruise and simply wanted more time with Caroline on Maui. Not only to solidify their friendship, but to show her how getting old didn't have to mean you had to stop living.

They had kept a slow pace on the island, long meals and luxurious naps. A tour to the vineyard and several afternoons on different beaches. Gracie had taught her how to navigate the genealogy website and Caroline was looking forward to delving deeper into her family history when she got home.

Both of the sisters taught Caroline how to steep the best cup of tea and how to pinch the most perfect Chinese dumplings. They'd taught her how to play Bridge, though Caroline wasn't that fond of it and probably wouldn't take it up. She'd learned some local words and how to give the hand signal *shaka* to show respect in town, though she felt silly doing it and made people laugh at every one of her attempts.

She'd learned that evenings don't need to be used up sitting in front of the television and that a bit of nature can cure a mile of maladies, but especially melancholy. That walking didn't need a destination and could be a wonderful time to reflect and discover the little things that being busy usually kept camouflaged in life.

They'd taught her how to crack a coconut, create a beautiful flower arrangement, and strum the ukulele enough to look like she really knew how to play it.

It was amazing how much they packed into one week without feeling like they were in any hurry whatsoever, and actually seemed to take their time about everything.

Island time, they called it.

The slow pace had changed when they flew back to the mainland. Even with the boot on and the occasional morning of pain, Betty had taken Caroline all over town, introducing her to people and different experiences.

San Francisco was amazing and Caroline was so glad she'd said yes.

The city seriously had everything you could think of.

"Come here, boy," Betty called out.

Her dog ran by, the bell on his collar ringing out as he jumped onto Betty's lap. Theo was a Yorkshire terrier and so small that he wore a bell to keep people from stepping on him. Having him around made her miss her cats and she hoped that Felix and Fauci hadn't forgotten her. More than likely, they'd snub their noses when she returned home, but after a few hours they'd forgive her. Just in case, though, she'd already picked up some of the fanciest cat treats money could buy from a cat café near Betty's house, and she planned on filling up her memory on her phone with pictures of them, as a consolation prize and something that James would find endearing.

Speaking of James, she had continued to find dimes in the most unlikely places and that told her that he would approve of her little California trip and all the ways she was getting out of her comfort zone to enjoy life.

Just the night before, a group of them had gone to a restaurant that offered an outstanding tasting menu complete with molecular cooking, something that Caroline wasn't even going to try to explain but had plenty of photos to show the girls.

Rachel was going to be especially interested in the exhibit that Betty had taken Caroline to at the Asian Art Museum. It had included more than a dozen movement-sensitive works that were hypersensitive to human activity. Caroline had been in awe of the darting fish and the gentle flutter of butterfly wings and couldn't wait to tell her youngest daughter all about it.

"And you're going to join a bowling league, right?" Betty asked her.

Caroline nodded. "I sure am and better than that, I'll have you know that I've already reached out to a friend of mine and she's going to join with me."

Fancy dinners and art museums were great, but Caroline was most excited about the simple things she'd discovered she liked. Bowling and book clubs, who would've ever thought it?

Some of Betty's friends tried to introduce Caroline to tennis and swimming, and she was glad they found it enjoyable, but it wasn't her thing.

Caroline wanted something to feel really passionate about. Painting, or volunteer work. Not tons of it, but just enough to give her something to feel responsible for. Her time away from home had given her time to think, and to remember that the happiest and most fulfilled people she'd known in life were the ones who had something profound to devote time to.

She was no martyr, though. She also planned on doing some fun things for herself.

Not that she was going to suddenly turn into a social butterfly and fill every evening, but starting small with bowling, or committing to reading and discussing a book once a month was something she could easily handle. If it led to more social things, so be it, but if it didn't, that was okay, too.

Laura and Peggy were already asking her to more family events, anyway, telling her to put them on her calendar. Rachel said they were going to do something together twice a month. Caroline was glad she'd told them how she really felt.

Suddenly her life was looking busy. Maybe too busy!

Caroline was also relieved that after the trip, Peggy had thrown her ego to the side and talked to her husband about counseling, and ways to make this transitional part of their life go smoother. She'd also asked Caroline's advice and really listened.

Sometimes her daughters forgot that she'd been through all the things they were juggling now, and she could tell them a bit about how to get through the busy years and then the strangeness of the empty nest stage.

Speaking of the girls, they'd made her so very proud, doing something totally unexpected on her behalf. The three of them had come together to donate money for a car for Betty's sister. It wasn't enough for a new car, but that wasn't necessary, and Gracie told them as much when she'd returned some after purchasing an older Nissan that she claimed was the exact car she'd been pining for the last few years.

Their gesture had alleviated Caroline's guilt over the accident and knowing her daughters were concerned about how she felt made it more special than they could know. They had also come together and had a series of heart-to-heart sisterly discussions about all the grievances they'd held against one another. Rachel confided that Peggy broke down and apologized for acting like a know-it-all and pledged to be kinder, and more honest about her shortcomings.

Caroline had souvenirs already packed for the grandkids, things like Muni t-shirts and hats with sketches of the trolleys on them, and vintage Levi's for the dads.

She missed them all so much, but she was grateful for the experience she'd had away. She was thankful they'd talked her into the cruise, too. Without taking the anniversary cruise, she would be in a totally different place now.

A very dark place, most likely.

Now Caroline knew the reality of it was that she'd probably grieve for James forever. She'd never get over losing him or their life together, but she'd learn to live with it, and she'd rebuild her life around his loss. The fact that she'd never be whole again without him was okay, too, because she would be herself, as much as she could be without being the person she was when he was still alive.

He was still around her, too. She didn't need any more dimes to show up and tell her that, though now it felt like the number ten was stalking her all over the place.

"Before tomorrow comes, Caroline, I want you to know I'm proud of you."

"Proud? For what?"

"You've come so far in the last few weeks when it comes to dealing with the loss of James."

Caroline took a deep breath. "Thank you, Betty. It's still just so hard. I don't know if I can keep it up or if my progress will be stunted when I get home and around his things again. It's easier here, because I don't see a memory in every corner."

"It is hard, indeed. I remember. It turns your world upside down and inside out and makes you feel naked in front of everyone you know and love. Your emotions are extreme, you find yourself getting angry at the stupidest things and forgetting to do some of the most important things.... then slowly, one day, the fog lifts a little and you see the brightness of joy again and little by little, your grief becomes a little bit lighter."

"I hope that day comes soon," Caroline said.

"It will. And at first, you'll feel guilty, but you are able to start claiming that joy as yours, especially as you lean into the arms of the One who loves you most. You have my number, and you are welcome to call or text me at any time. You will be in my constant prayers. I can tell you this for sure; you get stronger through these hard times of your life. Caroline, I see you as a fighter and an overcomer and you will look back one day and go, 'whoa, I made it.' Keep fighting my friend, keep fighting."

Caroline was so overcome with emotion that she

couldn't speak. Her life would be different now because of Betty and the friendship they'd built together. Betty understood what it was like to not only lose your husband, but to get old, to feel invisible and forgotten. Through it all, she'd learned how to stand up and be seen. And to enjoy life.

"Would it be weird for me to tell you I love you?" Caroline said softly.

Betty laughed. "It sure as heck wouldn't because I love you, too! Oh, and I nearly forgot," she said, pushing the recliner footrest closed and sitting forward. "Come with me." She led the way through the kitchen and out the back door to her small patio outside.

She took Caroline's arm, then pointed up into the sky.

"Look," she said.

"What am I looking for?" Caroline asked, squinting upward.

"See those stars? Get busy, friend. I want you to remember that you're never too old to wish on one. After all, no matter how much time you have left, there's still a lot of life to live. Getting older will wrinkle your skin and that's okay, but to keep from wrinkling your soul, hold on to your enthusiasm for life."

And that was the most valuable lesson that Caroline would take home with her.

If you enjoyed the cameo of Betty's sister, Gracie, in this story, she plays a much bigger role in my novel TRUE TO

ME that is a fan favorite. It's set on Maui and involves a family saga and mystery that will keep you turning pages. You can find that book on Amazon.

If you enjoyed sailing away with Caroline McClellan on Serenity of the Seas, you'll love cruising with Katie Torrey on her trip to the Eastern Caribbean in Moonlight on the Lido Deck by Violet Howe.

★ **Don't miss a Sail Away book!** ★
(All the books are standalones and can be read in any order.)

Book 1: Welcome Aboard – prologue book
Book 2: The Sound of the Sea by Jessie Newton
Book 3: Uncharted Waters by Tammy L. Grace
Book 4: A Not So Distant Shore by Ev Bishop
Book 5: Caroline, Adrift by Kay Bratt
Book 6: Moonlight on the Lido Deck by Violet Howe
Book 7: The Winning Tickets by Judith Keim
Book 8: Lost At Sea by Patricia Sands
Book 9: The Last Port of Call by Elizabeth Bromke

Thank You from the Author

Thank you so much for reading CAROLINE, ADRIFT, a standalone book in the SAIL AWAY series collaboration of bestselling authors. I've thoroughly enjoyed writing this story and hope that you've enjoyed reading it. Please forgive me for the liberties I took in making up the cruise line, ship, and itinerary, as well as different aspects of this fictional cruise to make it the story I needed to tell.

The idea for this book came about after I rebranded a Facebook group into a place for ladies of a certain age and place in their life to gather for support. Here's the introduction to the group: *Welcome to Midlife and Beyond; the weird place, after midlife but not dead yet. Together we are creating a judgment-free place to vent, laugh, and commiserate. This support group is for women of a certain age to find comfort with each other and tackle what comes next. Together, we'll navigate into the golden years with grace and wisdom, to find joy in the little things.*

Feel free to come visit me there, too!

While writing this book, I was interested to find in my research a study by the *New England Journal of Medicine* that determined the most productive age in human life is between sixty and seventy years old, and the second most productive is between seventy to eighty. More studies show that women are still being productive well into their eighties now! All this tells us that the best years of your life should be between sixty and ninety years old, and it's up to us to find a way to make that true. Obviously at that age you no longer have your youth or vitality in the physical aspect, but with your unlimited life experiences, you have so much more to offer than you think! If you are within those ages and find yourself stumbling along, I encourage you to search for a new purpose.

At the time of publishing this book I am fifty-three years old and I'm already curious about what my life will be like in my sixties, seventies, and beyond. If I'm still on this earth then, I hope I'll find ways to continue to enjoy life, feel productive and keep a positive perspective. I have spent much of my life in service to others in different avenues of volunteer work, and one day I plan to carve even more time out for philanthropic efforts that feed my passion.

My thanks go out to those in my Krew for always being the support I need, when I'm happy or sad, or when they are talking me out of committing a felony when it comes to rescuing dogs from backyard prison pens. (So far, I've managed to follow the law in my dog rescue endeavors, but you never know.)

A huge thank you to Pam Pool Kleiser for helping me get into the head of what a recent widow may feel like and giving me many of her words as counsel from Betty to Caroline. Sorry if this sounds weird, *but I love you, friend*.

To my first beta reader (and Caroline's namesake), Caroline Lynch, thanks for all your sound advice over the years and thanks for being first to read this story. Many thanks to Joy Lorton, the best proofreader out there. Kudos to both of you for embracing your age and continuing to stay busy and find ways to be happy. You are what I aspire to be one day!

Thank you to others in my Midlife & Beyond Facebook group for also participating in various question and answer sessions related to aging.

The lovely and successful Sophia Loren told us that "*There is a fountain of youth: it is your mind, your talents, the creativity you bring to your life and the lives of people you love. When you learn to tap this source, you will truly have defeated age.*" I am already tapping into that source and hope to continue doing so until the time that God calls me home.

If you have enjoyed CAROLINE, ADRIFT, I hope that you'll take the time to post a short review on Amazon, Goodreads, or BookBub. I also have many more books for you to choose from if you care to read more of my work. Thank you for your support.

See more titles at my website: https://kaybratt.com

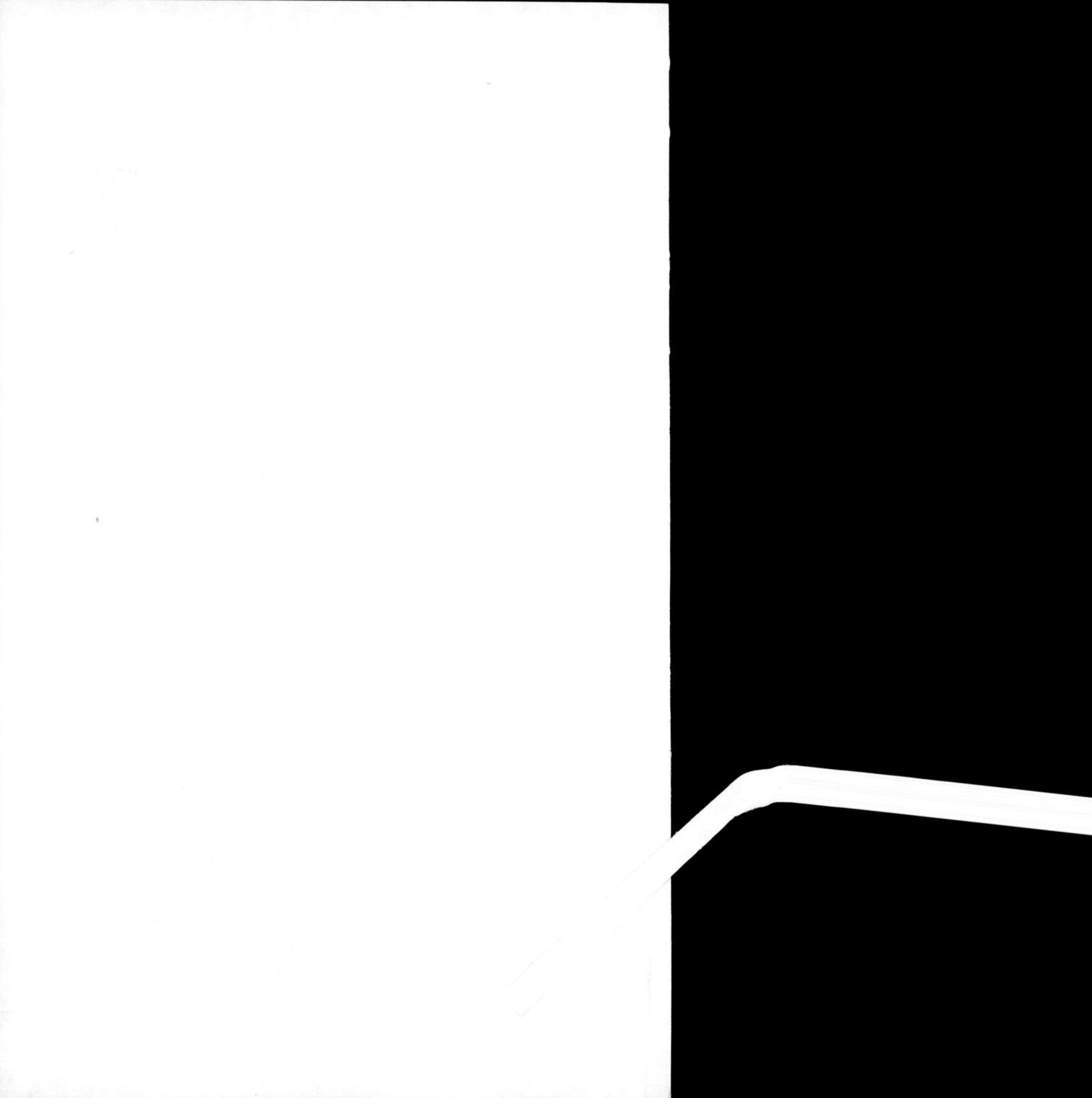

About the Author

Photo © 2021 Stephanie Crump Photography

Kay Bratt learned to lean on writing while she navigated a tumultuous childhood and then a decade of domestic abuse in adulthood. After working her way through the hard years to come out a survivor and a pursuer of peace, she finally found the courage to use her experiences throughout her novels, most recently *Wish Me Home* and *True to Me*. She lives with the love of her life and pack of rescue dogs on the banks of Lake Hartwell in Georgia, USA. For more information, visit www.kaybratt.com.